UNMASKING THE EVIL: THE TRUTH ABOUT NARCISSISTIC ABUSE

Understanding Narcissistic Abuse, Escaping Its Grip, and Embracing Healing.

SHWETA NEMA

ISBN
Paperback 979-8-89961-007-3
Hardcase 979-8-89961-008-0

This book has been published with all efforts taken to make the material error-free after the consent of the author. However, the author and the publisher do not assume and hereby disclaim any liability to any party for any loss, damage, or disruption caused by errors or omissions, whether such errors or omissions result from negligence, accident, or any other cause.

While every effort has been made to avoid any mistake or omission, this publication is being sold on the condition and understanding that neither the author nor the publishers or printers would be liable in any manner to any person by reason of any mistake or omission in this publication or for any action taken or omitted to be taken or advice rendered or accepted on the basis of this work. For any defect in printing or binding the publishers will be liable only to replace the defective copy by another copy of this work then available.

Dedication

To my daughter, your resilience and light have been my greatest source of strength. You are the reason I never gave up, and I dedicate this journey to you.

To my friends and loved ones who supported me in the toughest phase of my life.

CONTENTS

ACKNOWLEDGMENTS

To the experts in the field of Narcissism, your work has been invaluable in deepening my understanding of narcissistic personality disorder and its lasting impact.

To the divine force that guided me through the darkest storms, giving me the wisdom, courage, and clarity to break free.

To every survivor of narcissistic abuse who endured invalidation, hopelessness, and the suffocating trap of an abusive relationship, this book is for you.

This book is a recognition of what you survived, a call to awaken your spirit, and a guide to help you step onto the path of healing and freedom.

To the parents who fought fiercely to protect their children, even when it meant sacrificing their own dreams, and to those who carried the unbearable weight of survival while the world turned a blind eye, you are the true heroes.

INTRODUCTION

Imagine waking up every day feeling like you're walking on eggshells—measuring every word you say, anticipating every possible reaction and bracing for criticism or anger no matter how careful you are. Your thoughts feel tangled, your emotions suppressed, and your sense of self... fading. Even the smallest decisions seem monumental because, somehow, they're always wrong in someone else's eyes. This is the invisible prison built by narcissistic abuse.

For years, this was my reality. The subtle manipulations and constant undermining and criticism weren't always loud or obvious, but they were relentless. Simple moments; planning a vacation, pursuing my career, or even having time for a hobby—were turned into battles. Any attempt to assert independence or growth was subtly obstructed through, guilt trips, or outright sabotage.

Over time, I stopped trusting my instincts. I questioned everything about myself—Am I too sensitive? Am I overreacting? Is this my fault? This is the slow erosion narcissistic abuse creates. You become a shadow of yourself, doubting your own reality while navigating a maze of someone else's control.

And then there was the coercion. I was forced to leave a life I had built, enduring false accusations, fighting for the right to live peacefully with my child, and navigating the crushing weight of financial abuse. It wasn't just about the words or the manipulation—it was about the calculated efforts to strip me of my autonomy, control my resources, and leave me financially dependent and vulnerable. The coercion didn't just come from my spouse—it came from everywhere. It was a concerted effort to make me feel like I had no choice, no escape, and no support.

Even when I knew deep down that I was suffocating, I was told time and time again that this was just part of life. "Tough it out. It's not that bad. Things will get better. The manipulative message was clear—"Stay. Endure. Don't rock the boat."

Most survivors of narcissistic abuse find the first step of breaking free to be the hardest. The psychological web spun by a narcissist is designed to entrap, confuse, and make you doubt your own reality. This book is about untangling that web, reclaiming your sense of self, and ultimately breaking free, not just physically, but mentally and emotionally.

Why is escaping so difficult, and why is healing such a long and complicated process? Because narcissistic abuse is not just about manipulation or control—it's a deep psychological conditioning that rewires your brain to accept mistreatment as normal. It shatters your self-esteem, creates cognitive dissonance, and leaves you questioning your own worth. That's why the path to freedom isn't just about leaving, it's about unlearning, understanding, and rebuilding from the inside out.

But this book isn't just about the pain. It's about reclaiming your power. It's about understanding the abuse, recognizing it for what it is, and learning to navigate through the chaos with strength and clarity. Through awareness, you can break free from the grip of narcissistic abuse. And through spirituality, you can rebuild your sense of self, regain your peace, and reclaim the life that was stolen from you.

With each page, we'll uncover the truth about narcissism, the effects it has on your mind, body, and spirit, and how you can heal and move forward. This is your path to liberation—a path where your truth matters, your voice is heard, and your life is yours to live once again. You're not alone on this journey.

CHAPTER 1

WHAT IS NARCISSISTIC ABUSE?

Narcissistic abuse is a form of psychological manipulation that is often subtle, insidious, and difficult to detect at first. It involves the systematic undermining of another person's self-worth and identity by someone who demonstrates narcissistic traits. Unlike physical abuse, narcissistic abuse is covert, leaving no visible scars, but the emotional and psychological toll is far more devastating.

Narcissistic abuse is a pervasive, calculated form of manipulation that infiltrates every facet of a victim's life, leaving deep and often invisible scars. In this chapter, we define narcissistic abuse as not merely a series of isolated hurtful acts but as a systematic pattern of control and degradation. By exploring the underlying mechanisms and psychological impacts of these behaviors, this chapter aims to equip you with the knowledge to recognize and understand the true nature of narcissistic abuse.

Defining Narcissistic Abuse

A narcissist takes the time to deeply learn about you, your values, principles, likes, dislikes, relationships, and personal history. They gather this information not out of genuine interest, but to use it later for manipulation and control. Once they know your weaknesses and traumas, they begin to exploit them as weapons.

They bring up your insecurities or past wounds to trigger emotional pain, making you feel vulnerable and unworthy. They twist your words, distort your reality, and use your deepest fears to manipulate your emotions and decisions. This strategy ensures they maintain control while breaking down your confidence and leaving you doubting your own worth.

Through this process, they engage in dehumanization, stripping away your sense of self-worth and reducing you to a mere tool for their manipulation. Narcissists view their victims as objects, something to be used, discarded, or re-shaped to meet their needs. The emotional neglect and cruelty they inflict make you feel invisible, unimportant, and incapable of being valued by anyone. They systematically devalue you, dismissing your emotions, experiences, and humanity, turning you into a shadow of who you once were.

Narcissistic abuse often starts subtly and escalates over time. Early in the relationship, the abuser may be charming, attentive, and affectionate, which is often referred to as the "love-bombing" phase. As the relationship progresses, abusive behaviors gradually increase, making it hard to pinpoint when the relationship turned toxic.

Narcissists often operate from a deeply unconscious and fear-driven place, though they mask it with arrogance and control. Beneath their grandiosity lies a fragile ego, terrified of exposure and vulnerability. Their delusions are a shield, protecting them from the painful truth of their inadequacies, often stemming from unresolved wounds or unmet needs from their past.

They remain disconnected from genuine self-awareness, trapped in a cycle of projection and blame, unwilling or unable to confront their inner fears. Fear of rejection, failure, or losing control drives their manipulative behaviors, as they desperately try to maintain the illusion of superiority. Their delusion isn't just an act for others—it's a false reality they cling to, convincing themselves of their own narratives to avoid the discomfort of self-reflection.

This unconscious state makes them both dangerous and pitiable. They are blind to their destructiveness, not realizing that their attempts to dominate and control only deepen their inner emptiness and alienation.

Narcissistic abuse can occur in various relationships, including romantic partnerships, families, friendships, and workplaces. The effects on victims are profound, leading to anxiety, depression, low self-esteem, and complex emotional trauma, as they grapple with the manipulation and exploitation designed to sustain the abuser's sense of superiority and control.

Narcissists are seen as charming and successful, which helps them mask their true intentions. Their charm draws people in, using charisma, attentiveness, and humor to create strong connections. They appear driven and accomplished, meticulously curating an impressive public image. However, beneath this façade lies manipulation and exploitation, as they use others to maintain their status and control. Their charm and success make it harder for others to recognize the abuse they inflict behind closed doors.

NPD can be incredibly challenging to diagnose. The person with NPD flips the situation, turning the tables to confuse others and deflect attention from their behavior. A proper diagnosis should come from a specialist in NPD, as this condition can be subtle and deceptive. Individuals with NPD are highly skilled at masking their traits in public, presenting a charming façade while concealing their true nature. This makes it difficult for others to recognize the signs and understand the impact of their behavior.

Sometimes you'll find two narcissists working together to con someone. They may be best friends or even a couple. They feel comfortable with each other because they both lack morals, character and empathy. Make no mistake though that one of them is calling the shots and abusing the other while the weaker of the two knows that they are being degraded and tries even harder to be as devious as their master. Neither of them really like each other but they feel smart and secure in their sick and twisted world.

Narcissists engage in "introjection" and "projection", subconsciously adopting abusive behaviors they've experienced or witnessed somewhere and expecting others to act similarly. This stems from unresolved trauma and manifests as *"repetition compulsion"*, where they recreate familiar abusive dynamics. Their distorted belief system leads them to preemptively act out, projecting their fears or past pain onto others, perpetuating cycles of distrust and manipulation.

Unconscious behaviours often feel like they're your own, but in reality, they may be the result of strategic manipulation by someone with full-blown Narcissistic Personality Disorder (NPD). Over time, this manipulation can break your spirit and leave you emotionally paralyzed. Recovering from such abuse is a long process, especially for your nervous system.

Narcissists are skilled at projecting a polished, charming image to the outside world, making it difficult for others to see the abusive side that exists behind closed doors.

"Domestic violence is not just being hit, choked, slammed against a wall. Its also being disregarded, humiliated, blamed, screamed at, lied to, cheated on and controlled and held hostage. This is narcissistic abuse."

"Narcissists steal your ideas, money, people, energy and resources and refuse to credit you, they erase you and resend you for all the help you gave them and will destroy if you try to get the recognition you deserve."

Breaking down the Victim

Narcissistic abuse is far more than manipulation. It's a calculated campaign of destruction, fueled by an insatiable hunger for power and control. Every action they take is designed to dismantle you piece by piece until nothing remains of the person you once were. Whether it's your career, hobbies, relationships, or sense of self, nothing is off-limits. Their cruelty often feels inhuman, as though driven by a darkness that thrives on chaos and suffering.

A narcissist systematically dismantles a victim's self-worth through relentless criticism, targeting every aspect of their identity. They scrutinize your looks, your weight, skin, hair, or even the way you dress—planting insecurities where none existed. Your posture, the way you walk, or how you carry yourself becomes a point of mockery. They degrade your voice, your laugh, the way you express emotions, making you second-guess even natural behaviors.

Beyond physical traits, they attack your intelligence, skills, and abilities, making you feel incapable or unworthy. If you excel at something, they diminish it; if you struggle, they highlight your failures. Over time, these subtle but relentless criticisms strip away confidence, leaving you dependent on their validation, validation they never fully give.

Narcissists thrive on finding the perfect supply **empathetic, giving, and strong individuals** who they see as a challenge to conquer. Breaking down someone resilient feeds their sense of superiority far more than dominating someone weak. It starts subtly- they pretend to support your ambitions, taking pride in your talents and encouraging your passions. But as soon as they see how much joy or fulfillment these things bring you, their real motives surface.

They mock your hobbies, dismissing them as childish or a waste of time. They interrupt your quiet moments of creativity, pick fights when you're engrossed in something you love, and create distractions that prevent you from immersing yourself in your passions. Slowly but surely, they drain the joy from these activities, leaving you questioning their value. It's not that you lose interest—you simply associate your passions with their persistent negativity and abandon them altogether.

When it comes to your career, their sabotage becomes even more calculated. Independence threatens their control, and they know financial stability gives you an escape. They'll create chaos before important meetings, accuse you of prioritizing work over family, or conveniently "misplace" critical documents. They whisper doubts into your mind, convincing you that you're unworthy of success or that your ambitions are selfish. Sometimes, they'll manipulate you into **quitting your job entirely**, cloaking their control in the guise of love—**"You don't need to work, I'll take care of everything."** But once you're financially dependent, their true motives emerge. Money becomes a weapon, wielded to tighten their grip: **"You sit at home eating free food while I do everything. Why don't you start earning?"**

Their need for domination extends beyond your passions and career. They deliberately engineer situations designed to upset and provoke you. Imagine spending weeks planning a dinner party, only for them to swoop in at the last moment, taking credit for all your hard work. If you protest, they gaslight you into feeling ungrateful—***"Why are you making a scene? I'm just trying to help."***

The sabotage also targets your relationships. Narcissists are pathological liars, spinning webs of deceit to isolate you from your support system. They'll tell lies to your friends and family, painting you as unstable or difficult while portraying themselves as the victim. Over time, the rifts they create leave you with **no one** to lean on but them.

What makes this abuse so sinister is its intent. Every word, every action is deliberate, calculated to break your spirit and strip away your independence. ***It's not enough for them to win they need to see you lose.*** Their ultimate goal is to leave you powerless, dependent, and hollow, with no sense of identity or self-worth.

A narcissist will never give you the life you deserve. They won't even provide the bare minimum, all while knowing your strengths and worth. Instead, they'll systematically drain your *finances*, chip away at your *confidence*, and erode your *self-esteem*. They'll sabotage your *career*, launch a *smear campaign* to ruin your *reputation*, and work to crush your *spirit*. When they finally discard you, you're left deprived of everything you deserve, often struggling with mental health issues, potential autoimmune conditions, and the heavy responsibility of rebuilding stability for yourself and your children.

This destruction isn't accidental, it's methodical. They hate their partners most of all because a partner sees through their facade, witnessing their vulnerabilities and flaws. This exposure triggers deep resentment. To the narcissist, a partner becomes a constant reminder of the weaknesses they work so hard to hide, driving their need to dominate and destroy.

CHAPTER 2

RECOGNIZING NARCISSISTIC TRAITS

Understanding the signs of narcissistic behavior is essential for shielding yourself from emotional manipulation. Narcissists typically display an exaggerated sense of self-worth and a constant need for admiration, often neglecting or dismissing the feelings of those around them. They employ tactics such as gaslighting, twisting reality to erode your confidence and love bombing, which overwhelms you with attention only to later withdraw empathy. They also use subtler methods like backhanded compliments, the silent treatment, and triangulation to assert dominance and create confusion. By learning to identify these red flags early, you can establish healthy boundaries and take proactive steps to protect your emotional well-being.

Love Bombing: The Narcissist's Strategic Hook

Love bombing is one of the most manipulative and deceptive tactics narcissists use to gain control over their victims. It marks the initial phase of a narcissistic relationship, where the abuser showers their target with excessive affection, attention, and admiration. This overwhelming display of "love" creates a false sense of security and connection, making the victim feel unique, valued, and deeply bonded to the narcissist.

At first, love bombing feels like a fairy tale. The narcissist goes to extraordinary lengths; constant texting, extravagant gifts, lavish compliments, and promises of an ideal future. They mirror your dreams, values, and desires, making you believe you've found your soulmate. This phase is carefully designed to lower your defenses, intensifying your emotional investment in the relationship.

The Strategy Behind Love Bombing

During this intense period, the narcissist's goal is to create an emotional bond that will make you feel seen and appreciated. The constant praise, attention, and validation make you feel cherished, forming a powerful emotional attachment. The excitement of being constantly sought after triggers feel-good hormones like dopamine, creating a euphoric "high" that becomes addictive. Their promises of an ideal future convince you that you've found something special and worth holding onto, regardless of any red flags.

However, this phase is not about genuine love—it's a calculated strategy to gain control. Once the narcissist feels they've secured your trust and affection, the dynamic shifts abruptly.

Impact on the victim

Victims are left questioning which version of the narcissist is real—the loving, ideal partner or the cold, abusive one. The narcissist's approval becomes the victim's primary source of self-worth, making it difficult to imagine life without them. Narcissists often use guilt, fear, and manipulation to make their victims feel responsible for the relationship's problems, further entrenching the bond.

Hoping for change victims cling to the belief that the loving version of the narcissist will return if they just try harder. The narcissist conditions their victim to fear losing the "special connection" they once shared. Narcissists isolate their victims from friends and family, making it harder to seek help or leave.

Narcissists create dependency by breaking down their target's autonomy and isolating them. Initially, they use love-bombing to gain trust and affection, then erode self-esteem through gaslighting, criticism, and manipulation. They isolate the target from their support network, control finances, and create a cycle of fear, anxiety, and intermittent reinforcement to make the target feel helpless without them.

Simultaneously, they craft a false narrative to family and friends, portraying themselves as the victim and their target as the abuser. They spread lies, distort events, and use charm to gain sympathy, ensuring the target appears unreasonable or toxic. This isolates the target further, leaving them without allies and reinforcing their dependence on the narcissist.

Survivor Story:

When Sarah first met Daniel, he seemed like everything she had ever dreamed of; attentive, caring, and the perfect gentleman. He listened intently, took her to the doctor when she wasn't feeling well, and made her feel as if she was the center of his world. What she didn't realize was that this kindness was merely a façade, concealing his addictions and darker tendencies.

After they got married, the loving man she had fallen for began to vanish. In his place emerged someone cold, dismissive, and increasingly abusive. Yet, just when she felt ready to leave, he would suddenly overwhelm her with gifts and heartfelt apologies, insisting, "I only get upset because I care so much." These gestures reignited her hope, keeping her ensnared in a relentless cycle of pain and manipulation.

Only in hindsight did Sarah recognize that those early displays of affection were never genuine—they were merely calculated tactics to pull her in.

"While love bombing may feel like the beginning of a fairytale, it's a calculated tool designed to manipulate and control. Recognizing the signs can help you protect yourself from falling into a narcissist's trap and take the first steps toward freedom."

Grandiosity: The Inflated Sense of Self in Narcissism

Grandiosity is a hallmark trait of narcissistic personality disorder (NPD), characterized by an exaggerated sense of superiority, entitlement, and self-importance. Narcissists exhibit grandiosity to project an image of perfection, power, and invulnerability. This behavior not only reinforces their inflated self-view but also serves as a shield to mask their deep-seated insecurities. Narcissists are driven by deep-rooted insecurities and a fragile sense of self-worth. They construct a grandiose, self-assured exterior to mask their inner fears of inadequacy, rejection, and failure. To protect this false self-image, they use *projection*—a defense mechanism that involves displacing their insecurities onto those closest to them, often their spouse.

Grandiosity manifests as an overblown perception of one's abilities, achievements, or importance. Narcissists believe they are exceptional and deserving of admiration, even when there is little evidence to support their claims. This exaggerated self-image often leads them to demand special treatment, dismiss the needs of others, and overestimate their own influence or talents.

Narcissists inflate their accomplishments, claiming to be more successful or talented than they are. They expect preferential treatment, believing that rules and norms apply to others but not to them. Narcissists often daydream about unlimited success, power, or admiration, which they see as their birthright. They belittle or invalidate others' contributions, viewing them as inferior or irrelevant.

The Strategy Behind Grandiosity

Grandiosity is not just a display of arrogance—it is a calculated defense mechanism to maintain the narcissist's fragile self-esteem and control over others. Beneath the grandiose facade lies deep insecurity and fear of inadequacy. By exaggerating their importance, narcissists protect themselves from feelings of vulnerability or failure. Grandiosity serves as a magnet for attention and validation. Narcissists rely on others to bolster their self-worth, using their perceived superiority to command admiration. By presenting themselves as the most important or capable person in the room, narcissists establish control and discourage others from challenging them. Grandiosity allows narcissists to sidestep responsibility for their mistakes or flaws. They may deflect criticism by claiming that others are simply "jealous" or "unworthy" of their time.

The Impact on Victims

The grandiosity of a narcissist profoundly affects those around them, particularly in close relationships, where their inflated sense of self overshadows the victim's needs and emotions. Constant comparisons to the narcissist's exaggerated achievements can make victims feel inadequate or insignificant. The narcissist's obsession with their own greatness leaves little room for empathy or consideration of the victim's feelings, leading to emotional neglect. The narcissist's dismissal of the victim's accomplishments or ideas erodes the victim's confidence and self-worth. Grandiosity enables the narcissist to dominate conversations, decisions, and relationships, leaving the victim feeling powerless or silenced. The narcissist's grandiose fantasies can distort reality, causing the victim to doubt their own perceptions or believe the narcissist's inflated version of events.

For the narcissist, grandiosity is not just a personality trait—it is a survival strategy. It allows them to maintain a sense of superiority, secure validation, and avoid confronting their underlying insecurities.

> *"For the victim, understanding grandiosity as a defense mechanism rather than a genuine reflection of the narcissist's capabilities is crucial. Recognizing the behavior for what it is can help victims reclaim their sense of reality and self-worth, breaking free from the narcissist's overwhelming shadow."*

Survivor Story:

Daniel was a master of illusion, crafting a perfect image while doing the bare minimum behind closed doors. He thrived on taking credit for the efforts of others, all to uphold his grandiose self-image. Inside the house, he refused to lift a finger. Cleaning up messes, planning dinner parties, ensuring their child was fed and cared for—everything fell on Sarah's shoulders. Yet, the moment the doorbell rang and their guests arrived, he transformed.

Suddenly, he was the perfect host, beaming with pride as he boasted about the meal on the table as if he had prepared it himself. He poured wine, cracked jokes, and exuded charm, soaking in the admiration of their friends and family. No one saw the chaos that had unfolded just hours before—Sarah frantically cleaning, cooking, and making sure everything was perfect while Daniel lounged on the couch, scrolling through his phone or napping, oblivious to her exhaustion.

One evening, during a dinner party he had insisted on hosting, Sarah overheard him tell a guest, "It's all my hard work." Her stomach tightened as she fought the urge to correct him, swallowing her frustration instead. The truth was, she had single-handedly done everything while he barely acknowledged her efforts.

This charade of taking credit for her work wasn't limited to social gatherings— it defined their life together. Every decision Sarah made, whether for their child or the household, was met with criticism and ridicule. "You should have asked me first," Daniel would say smugly, as though she was incapable of making choices on her own.

Over time, Sarah began to doubt herself. Could she really not get anything right? Was she as incompetent as he made her feel? His constant belittling seeped into her mind like poison, eroding her confidence and amplifying her anxiety. What she didn't realize then was that this had been his intention all along—to elevate himself by making her feel small.

Yet, to the outside world, Daniel played the role of the devoted husband and father flawlessly. Looking back, Sarah could now see how his grandiosity was nothing more than a mask, concealing the emptiness beneath. He never cared about the effort she put into keeping their home running or the sacrifices she made. **The only thing that mattered to him was the applause he received for a performance he had never earned.**

Lack of Empathy: The Core of Narcissistic Personality Disorder

A narcissist's lack of empathy is nothing short of brutal, almost inhuman. While they may initially disguise themselves as caring and kind during the love-bombing phase, their true nature eventually surfaces, leaving a trail of cold indifference and callousness.

When you're unwell, hurt, or in desperate need of support, their response is icy and dismissive. They won't ask if you've eaten, offer you water, or care if you're struggling to get out of bed. Even their own sick child is met with apathy—they'll belittle the situation as "drama" or completely ignore it. It's as if your pain is invisible, irrelevant, or worse, an inconvenience to their self-absorbed existence.

But when the tables turn, and they're the ones unwell, it's an entirely different story. They will act as if the world is ending, demanding unwavering attention and sympathy. A slight cold is treated like a life-threatening illness, and their theatrics ensure everyone around them is catering to their needs. The sheer hypocrisy is staggering—a cruel reminder of just how little they value anyone but themselves.

To make matters worse, the narcissist plays a sinister game with the outside world. To everyone else, they are the picture-perfect gentleman, the one who's always there to lend a helping hand to friends and relatives. They go out of their way to appear generous and charming, cultivating an image that's so convincing it makes them untouchable.

This is where the real cruelty lies—if you dare to speak out about the abuse you endure behind closed doors, you'll be met with disbelief, ridicule, and accusations of lying. The people you turn to for help will defend the narcissist, invalidating your pain and painting you as unstable or vindictive. It's a masterful manipulation, designed to isolate you further and make you question your reality.

The duality of their public charm and private cruelty is no accident—it's a deliberate, calculated weapon to protect their image while ensuring you remain trapped, voiceless, and discredited. It's not just indifference—it's emotional warfare.

The Strategy Behind the Lack of Empathy

The lack of empathy exhibited by narcissists is not just a personality flaw—it's a calculated strategy designed to maintain control, manipulate others, and serve their own interests. While their indifference to others' feelings might appear to be a natural consequence of their self-centered nature, it is often a deliberate tool in their arsenal of emotional abuse.

By disregarding the feelings, needs, and well-being of others, narcissists create an emotional distance that allows them to manipulate without guilt or remorse. They see people not as individuals with their own thoughts and emotions but as objects to be used for their benefit. This dehumanization enables them to justify their cruel behaviour without internal conflict.

When a narcissist ignores your pain or dismisses your needs, it sends a clear message: **Your feelings don't matter.** This creates a power dynamic where the victim is left constantly seeking approval or acknowledgment, making them easier to control. The more you try to win their care or concern, the more power they hold over you.

By withholding empathy and emotional support, narcissists condition their victims to accept less and less over time. The lack of validation and care creates a deep sense of dependency, where any small act of attention from the narcissist feels like a reward. This is a form of psychological conditioning that strengthens the trauma bond, making it harder for victims to leave.

When victims express their pain, narcissists exploit it to their advantage. Instead of offering comfort, they might mock, belittle, or accuse the victim of being dramatic. This not only invalidates the victim's feelings but also teaches them that vulnerability will be met with cruelty, not compassion. Over time, this keeps the victim silent and compliant.

The lack of empathy is a key part of the narcissist's double life. In private, they show coldness and indifference to their victims, but in public, they portray themselves as compassionate and supportive individuals. This contrast ensures that if the victim speaks out, their claims will seem unbelievable to outsiders. The narcissist's indifference in private isolates the victim emotionally, while their public persona isolates the victim socially.

Empathy often requires acknowledgment of wrongdoing or responsibility, something a narcissist is unwilling to do. By refusing to care about the impact of their actions, they deflect blame and avoid accountability. They twist situations to make the victim feel at fault, further reinforcing their control.

Empathy requires vulnerability—a willingness to connect with another person's feelings. For a narcissist, vulnerability is seen as weakness. By rejecting empathy, they protect their fragile ego and maintain the illusion of superiority. To them, showing care or concern would mean lowering themselves, something their grandiose self-image cannot allow.

Impact on the Victim

For the victim, the lack of empathy feels like a soul—crushing void. It invalidates their humanity, isolates them from support, and keeps them trapped in a cycle of seeking validation from someone incapable of giving it. For the narcissist, this strategy ensures they remain in control, shielded from accountability, and free to manipulate without consequence.

The lack of empathy is not just indifference—it's a calculated move in the narcissist's game of power and control, designed to break the spirit of their victims while fortifying their own dominance.

A narcissist's lack of empathy can feel like a bottomless void, but you don't have to live within it. By understanding this key trait of NPD, you can begin to break free from their influence and reclaim your emotional autonomy.

"Understanding the narcissist's lack of empathy is a critical step in freeing yourself from their manipulation. Recognize that their indifference is not a reflection of your worth but a limitation within them."

Survivor Story:

When Sarah became pregnant, the neglect she had long endured took on a new form—one that left her completely isolated. The day she went into labor, the pain was relentless. She was induced, enduring hours of agony. Just before delivery, an epidural was administered, allowing her a brief moment of rest. When she woke up, Daniel was gone. Without a word, he had left her to face childbirth alone.

His absence during such a critical moment was only the beginning. Soon after, his family arrived, accompanied by two maids from their hometown, and took over their home for the next two months. Rather than offering support, her mother-in-law made endless demands, often stirring conflict over the smallest of matters. Sarah, still recovering, was expected to cook and serve them, despite her exhaustion. When her own mother came to care for her and the baby, she was sent away.

From that moment on, Sarah was left to fend for herself. No one asked if she needed food or water. She breastfed her newborn on an empty stomach while meals were prepared exclusively for Daniel and his family. The contrast was stark—while they dined comfortably, she was left unseen, her needs disregarded.

Despite this, Daniel found reason to complain—not about the burdens placed on Sarah, but about the cost of her medical care. Yet, the constant spending on his family's comforts was never questioned. Their indulgences were justified, but his wife's well-being was not.

Then came the moment that shattered any illusion of safety. One evening, as Sarah sat cradling her baby, Daniel erupted in rage. His father had visited, and the housemaid had arrived late—minor grievances that, in his eyes, warranted fury. Without hesitation, he grabbed Sarah by the throat and choked her. No remorse. No concern for her or their child. Just cold, calculated aggression.

This was not mere neglect—it was something far more insidious. A deliberate stripping away of dignity, a refusal to acknowledge her as a person with needs, emotions, or even basic rights. In that moment, the reality became undeniable: Sarah was not a partner, not a mother to be cherished, but a presence to be controlled, disregarded, and discarded at will.

Gaslighting: Manipulating Reality to Control and Undermine

In narcissistic abuse, gaslighting is a manipulative tactic that the narcissist uses to distort the victim's reality, making them question their own memory, perception, and sanity. Similar to love bombing, gaslighting is a subtle and insidious tactic that undermines the victim's confidence and self-trust, progressively making them dependent on the narcissist's version of events and reality.

At the beginning, the narcissist may dismiss or deny facts, even when the victim is certain about something. Common phrases like, **"That never happened"** or **"You're just imagining things"** are used to create doubt and confusion, causing the victim to question their memory. The narcissist's goal is to slowly erode the victim's sense of self, planting seeds of uncertainty that grow over time.

As the manipulation deepens, the narcissist escalates this behaviour, turning even small disagreements or misunderstandings into major distortions. They might accuse the victim of being "too sensitive" or "overreacting," which shifts the focus away from the narcissist's behaviour and places the blame squarely on the victim. This constant invalidation gradually erodes the victim's confidence in their own judgment, making them more reliant on the narcissist's false narrative.

Eventually, gaslighting leads the victim to question everything, from their thoughts to their memories, leaving them feeling mentally unstable and isolated. This psychological abuse not only destabilizes the victim's perception of reality but also deepens their emotional dependence on the narcissist, making it even harder for them to recognize the manipulation or escape the relationship.

The Strategy Behind Gaslighting

The goal of gaslighting is not just to confuse, but to make the victim feel insane or untrustworthy. The narcissist slowly conditions the victim into accepting their fabricated reality as the truth. It isolates them emotionally, because they no longer trust their own judgment, and it allows the narcissist to maintain control over every aspect of the relationship, keeping the victim in a constant state of uncertainty and dependence.

Impact on Victim

Gaslighting can be emotionally crippling, as the victim becomes increasingly isolated from their own intuition and perceptions. The narcissist may even turn others against the victim by planting seeds of doubt, reinforcing their grip on power. This systematic manipulation ensures that the victim stays confused, vulnerable, and reliant on the narcissist for validation and clarity.

Ultimately, gaslighting is about power and control. The narcissist uses it to distort the victim's reality, create confusion, and undermine their self-worth, leaving them trapped in a cycle of self-doubt and dependency.

"These psychological effects don't occur in isolation—they feed into each other, creating a web of emotional and mental paralysis. By the time the victim recognizes the gaslighting, they may feel too confused and powerless to fight back. Understanding these impacts is key to breaking free and reclaiming their sense of reality and self-worth."

Survivor Story:

Throughout her relationship with Daniel, gaslighting became a relentless weapon used to dismantle Sarah's sense of reality. The verbal abuse she endured was often denied outright, when she confronted him about the cruel things he had said. Words that still echoed painfully in her mind—he would dismiss her without hesitation.

"I never said that," Daniel would claim, his voice calm and unwavering. "You're just making things up." If she tried to recall specific instances, he would confidently insist that she didn't remember things correctly. His denials weren't just lies—they were direct attacks on her sanity. Each time he rejected the truth, he planted another seed of doubt in her mind, making her question her own perception.

He invalidated her feelings at every turn, making her believe that everything she was experiencing was imagined. If she expressed hurt or frustration, Daniel would accuse her of being overly dramatic or "too sensitive." The blame was always redirected onto her, as though her emotions were the real problem—not his behavior.

Over time, he twisted every conversation, every action, until Sarah found herself trapped in a distorted world where nothing she said made sense anymore—except in the version of reality Daniel had constructed, where she was always the problem.

The most insidious part was how his denials and accusations were often paired with cold, punishing silence. The longer she was met with indifference, the more she began to doubt herself. Slowly, her confidence in her own memories and experiences crumbled. The gaslighting was a slow, suffocating force that pulled her deeper into uncertainty, making her question whether she was ever truly in control of her reality. Each lie, each manipulation, pushed her further into a space where she couldn't even trust her own thoughts—until she found herself utterly dependent on him for validation and the so-called "truth."

Triangulation: A Tool of Division and Control

In narcissistic abuse, triangulation is a calculated strategy used by the narcissist to manipulate relationships, sow discord, and maintain control over their victim. This tactic involves introducing a third party—be it another person, a group, or even an abstract idea—into the dynamic to create competition, jealousy, and confusion. This involves pulling in third parties (friends, family members, or even strangers) to reinforce their version of events. Narcissists often manipulate these third parties, known as "flying monkeys," to pressure the victim into doubting their own perspective.

At its core, triangulation is a way for narcissists to control their environment by positioning themselves at the center of conflict. They craft a triangle where the victim feels pitted against a third party, while the narcissist plays the role of the authority, peacekeeper, or victim.

The Strategy Behind Triangulation

For the narcissist, triangulation is a powerful tool to **destabilize** the victim, create division, and assert dominance. By keeping the victim in a state of competition and insecurity, the narcissist strengthens their grip on the relationship, ensuring that the victim remains dependent, confused, and emotionally tethered.

By comparing the victim to someone else, the narcissist creates a sense of rivalry. The victim becomes preoccupied with trying to measure up or outdo the third party, diverting attention from the narcissist's behavior. The narcissist uses triangulation to create mistrust and division. They spread lies or play favorites, ensuring that the victim feels alienated and unsupported. The constant manipulation leaves the victim in a state of anxiety and confusion, making it harder for them to see the narcissist's true motives or actions. By controlling the narrative and being the central figure in the triangle, the narcissist ensures that they remain indispensable to both the victim and the third party.

The Impact on the Victim

Triangulation leaves deep psychological scars on the victim, impacting their self-esteem, relationships, and mental health. Constant comparisons or the presence of a third party make the victim feel inadequate or replaceable. The shifting narratives and conflicting stories lead the victim to question their own judgment, making them increasingly dependent on the narcissist for clarity and validation. As mistrust grows, the victim may withdraw from the third party or others, leaving them emotionally and socially isolated. The victim lives in a constant state of stress, trying to decipher the narcissist's motives, mend relationships, or win back their favor. Over time, the victim internalizes the belief that they are not good enough, smart enough, or worthy of love, based on the narcissist's manipulative comparisons.

> *"Triangulation is not just a tactic of control- it's a deliberate act of sabotage that fractures trust, relationships, and the victim's sense of self."*

Survivor Story:

During their marriage, Daniel weaponized triangulation as one of the most painful and manipulative tactics to control and break Sarah. But he didn't act alone—he involved others, particularly her own sister, using their close bond against her.

He would speak to Sarah's sister behind her back, distorting events and twisting the truth to make Sarah seem unreasonable, overly emotional, or unstable.

With careful manipulation, he painted himself as the rational, patient husband struggling to deal with an impossible wife. He knew exactly how to exploit emotions, gradually turning her sister into his ally.

Over time, Sarah noticed a shift in how her sister treated her. The words that once felt supportive now mirrored Daniel's criticisms. "You're always so difficult," her sister would say, or "Why can't you just get along with him?" Each phrase felt eerily familiar, echoing his complaints almost word for word. It became clear that, knowingly or unknowingly, her sister had been pulled into his web of deception.

The most painful part was how Daniel used these comparisons to tear Sarah down. During arguments, he would pit them against each other, smirking as he said, "Why can't you be more like your sister? She's so calm and understanding, and you're always making a scene." No matter what Sarah did, she could never measure up in his eyes. It wasn't about genuine praise for her sister—it was about making Sarah feel inferior, highlighting her perceived flaws while elevating someone else as the standard she could never reach.

This manipulation left Sarah feeling isolated and helpless. It wasn't just Daniel gaslighting her anymore—he had orchestrated a dynamic where even her own sister unknowingly became part of his game. Every argument, every confrontation, felt like a setup—another opportunity for him to belittle her, to force her into apologizing for things that weren't her fault.

With time, he created an environment where Sarah was always the villain. He played the innocent victim flawlessly, deflecting blame while ensuring she was the one constantly scrutinized. When she tried to stand up for herself, she was met with accusations of overreacting, and her sister now caught in his manipulation, would reinforce those claims.

As Sarah watched her relationship with her sister deteriorate, she realized just how deeply he had embedded himself into every aspect of her life. He had turned her support system against her, leaving her utterly alone in a storm he had carefully engineered.

Silent Treatment: A Weapon of Emotional Punishment

The silent treatment is a common tactic used by narcissists to manipulate, punish, and control their victims. By withdrawing communication, attention, or affection, the narcissist creates an atmosphere of emotional tension and confusion. This behavior is not merely passive-aggressive—it is a deliberate strategy aimed at maintaining dominance and leaving the victim feeling isolated and powerless.

Silent treatment occurs when a narcissist intentionally ignores or stonewalls the victim, refusing to engage in conversations, respond to messages, or acknowledge their presence. This tactic can last for hours, days, or even weeks, depending on the narcissist's goal.

Unlike a healthy timeout used to cool off during disagreements, the narcissist's silent treatment is a calculated act meant to punish or provoke a reaction from the victim.

The Strategy Behind Silent Treatment

The silent treatment serves as a powerful weapon in the narcissist's arsenal for several reasons. The silent treatment is not about resolution—it's about control. By weaponizing silence, the narcissist reinforces their dominance while eroding the victim's emotional resilience.

If the victim challenges the narcissist's authority, sets boundaries, or fails to meet their expectations, the silent treatment is used as retribution. By withholding communication, the narcissist places themselves in a position of power, forcing the victim to make the first move to restore harmony. The sudden withdrawal of attention leaves the victim feeling confused, anxious, and desperate for resolution, making them more pliable to the narcissist's demands. Silent treatment is a convenient way for the narcissist to avoid addressing conflicts, shifting the blame onto the victim while escaping responsibility for their actions. The narcissist often hopes that the victim will become distressed or angry, allowing the narcissist to portray themselves as the victim of the situation.

The Impact on the Victim

The silent treatment is a form of emotional abuse that can have severe psychological consequences for the victim. Being ignored makes the victim feel unworthy of attention or acknowledgment, leading to feelings of rejection and self-doubt. The unpredictability of the silent treatment creates a state of constant tension, as the victim struggles to understand what went wrong and how to fix it. The narcissist's refusal to engage sends a message that the victim's feelings and needs are irrelevant, damaging their sense of self-esteem. The silence drives the victim to overcompensate by apologizing, appeasing, or taking responsibility for things they didn't do. Over time, the victim may withdraw from others, internalizing the belief that they are at fault and that the silent treatment is a justified response to their actions.

> *"For the victim, recognizing the silent treatment as a manipulative tactic rather than a reflection of their worth is key. Establishing firm boundaries and refusing to play into the narcissist's game are essential steps in breaking free from this cycle of emotional abuse."*

Survivor Story:

It started with something as trivial as an opinion. Sarah had voiced her thoughts on a simple matter—she preferred a quiet evening at home instead of Daniel's last-minute plans to host friends. It wasn't a refusal, just a suggestion. But in Daniel's world, disagreement wasn't an option.

What followed was an unbearable silence. No words, no acknowledgment of her presence— just a cold, deliberate withdrawal. At first, Sarah assumed he needed space, time to process his frustration. But hours turned into a day, and a day stretched into two. Every attempt she made to bridge the gap was met with stone-cold indifference.

When she apologized—despite not understanding what she had done wrong—her words fell into a void. He refused to respond, leaving the house heavy with an unspoken tension that made every moment suffocating. Sarah walked on eggshells, replaying the disagreement over and over in her mind, desperately trying to pinpoint the "mistake" that had warranted such punishment.

It became a pattern. Anytime she expressed an opinion he didn't like, challenged his ideas, or dared to say "no," the silent treatment would descend like a shadow. It was his weapon of choice—an invisible wound that cut deep into her self-worth. Slowly, she began to doubt the value of her voice, her thoughts, and even her presence in the relationship.

She learned to comply. To stay silent. To agree even when she didn't want to. Her opinions no longer mattered—only keeping the peace did. Avoiding the void of his silence became her priority.

What Sarah didn't realize then was that his silence had never been about an argument or a simple disagreement. It had always been about control. The silent treatment wasn't a lack of communication—it was a deliberate strategy to assert dominance, to make her feel invisible and powerless until she submitted. Looking back, she saw it for what it was—emotional abuse.

DARVO: A manipulation Tactic

DARVO is an acronym that stands for Deny, Attack, and Reverse Victim and Offender. It is a psychological manipulation tactic often used by narcissists, abusers, and toxic individuals to deflect responsibility and shift blame onto the victim. This tactic is particularly common in narcissistic relationships, workplace conflicts, and legal disputes where the abuser wants to avoid accountability.

Deny – The narcissist outright denies any wrongdoing.

- "I never said that."
- "That never happened."
- "You're imagining things."
- "You're being too sensitive."

The goal is to confuse the victim and make them doubt their own perception of reality (gaslighting).

Attack – Instead of addressing the issue, they attack the victim's character.

- "You're the problem, not me!"
- "You're crazy and overreacting."
- "You're the one causing drama."

The goal here is to intimidate, silence, or discredit the victim so they feel too guilty or ashamed to continue defending themselves.

Reverse Victim and Offender – The abuser flips the roles, portraying themselves as the victim and making the real victim look like the aggressor.

- "You're the one hurting me!"
- "I can't believe you're treating me this way after everything I've done for you!"
- "Now you're attacking me? I'm the one suffering!"

The goal is to gain sympathy from others, manipulate the narrative, and make the real victim feel guilty for standing up for themselves.

CHAPTER 3

Understanding "Narcissistic Personality Disorder"

Narcissism, a term that has permeated popular culture and psychological discourse, is often misunderstood and oversimplified. At its core, narcissism is a personality trait characterized by a grandiose sense of self-importance, a deep need for admiration, and a lack of empathy for others. While everyone may exhibit narcissistic traits to some extent, especially in certain situations or phases of life, it becomes a concern when these traits are pervasive, rigid, and lead to significant impairment or distress.

The concept of narcissism has its roots in Greek mythology, where the story of Narcissus, a young man who fell in love with his own reflection, serves as a cautionary tale about self-obsession. In psychological terms, narcissism was first extensively explored by Sigmund Freud, who described it as a normal stage of development. However, when individuals fail to move beyond this stage, they may develop what is now recognized as narcissistic personality disorder (NPD).

Narcissistic personality disorder is classified in the Diagnostic and Statistical Manual of Mental Disorders (DSM-5) as a cluster B personality disorder, which is characterized by dramatic, emotional, or erratic behaviors. Individuals with NPD often display an exaggerated sense of self-importance, preoccupation with fantasies of unlimited success or power, and a belief that they are special and unique. They may require excessive admiration, believe they are entitled to special treatment, and exploit others to achieve their own ends.

Despite the air of confidence and superiority that narcissistic individuals project, underlying these traits is often a fragile self-esteem. This fragility makes them highly sensitive to criticism or perceived slights, often resulting in intense emotional reactions or vindictive behaviors. Furthermore, their lack of empathy can lead to difficulties in forming and maintaining healthy relationships, as they struggle to recognize or respect the feelings and needs of others.

It is important to distinguish between healthy narcissism and pathological narcissism. Healthy narcissism can be beneficial, contributing to self-confidence, ambition, and resilience. **Pathological narcissism**, however, is maladaptive and can lead to significant disruptions in an individual's personal and professional life. This distinction is crucial in understanding and addressing narcissistic behavior, particularly in the context of narcissistic abuse.

Narcissistic abuse is a form of emotional and psychological abuse perpetrated by individuals with narcissistic traits or NPD. It often involves manipulation, gaslighting, financial abuse and control leaving victims feeling confused, worthless, and emotionally drained. Understanding the nuances of narcissism is essential for recognizing the signs of narcissistic abuse and taking steps to protect oneself from its damaging effects.

Origins and Causes

Narcissism doesn't develop in isolation. It emerges from a complex interplay of genetic, environmental, and psychological factors that shape personality development. Understanding these origins provides insight into why narcissists behave the way they do and how their traits manifest.

Narcissistic traits often originate in **childhood experiences**. Parenting styles, emotional neglect, or trauma during formative years can significantly impact a child's self-perception and relationships. A child who is excessively praised for achievements without acknowledgment of their inner self may develop a sense of entitlement, while constant criticism or belittlement can lead to fragile self-esteem masked by arrogance. Growing up in an environment where emotional needs are ignored may push a child to seek validation externally.

Overindulgent parents can foster unrealistic expectations of admiration, whereas overprotective parenting can create a fear of failure and dependency on external validation.

Traumatic experiences, such as emotional, physical, or sexual abuse, can contribute to the development of narcissistic defenses. These individuals may construct an exaggerated self-image to cope with feelings of vulnerability, fear, or worthlessness. Narcissistic traits may function as a survival mechanism, shielding against feelings of inadequacy or suppressing painful memories. Disrupted attachment to caregivers in early childhood can result in difficulty forming healthy relationships and a lack of empathy.

Biological factors also play a role. Genetic predisposition and neurobiology influence the likelihood of narcissistic tendencies. Research suggests that inherited personality traits, such as impulsivity or low agreeableness, may increase the risk. Differences in brain structure, particularly in areas related to empathy, emotional regulation, and reward processing, have been observed in individuals with narcissistic personality disorder (NPD). These neurological differences contribute to their inability or unwillingness to form deep emotional connections or regulate their need for admiration and control.

Cultural and societal influences further shape narcissistic behaviors. In cultures that emphasize individualism and competitiveness, narcissistic traits may be more prevalent. Modern society often glorifies ambition, beauty, and success, reinforcing self-centered behaviors. The rise of social media, where self-promotion is rewarded with likes and followers, can amplify narcissistic tendencies, particularly in vulnerable individuals.

Narcissism can also function as a **psychological defense mechanism** to protect against deeper wounds. Behind the façade of confidence, many narcissists struggle with insecurity and fear of rejection. Their need for control and dominance often stems from a fear of being emotionally exposed or hurt.

Understanding the deliberate nature of their harm—While narcissism is shaped by genetics and experiences, it is crucial to recognize that individuals with NPD are not cognitively impaired. **They fully understand the harm their**

actions cause and intentionally choose these behaviors. Their manipulation, gaslighting, and emotional abuse are not accidental but calculated strategies to maintain control over others. The harm they inflict is deliberate, not a result of confusion or misunderstanding.

It's important to note that no single factor causes narcissism. It arises from a combination of influences that shape an individual's personality and coping mechanisms. While these origins don't justify abusive behaviors, understanding them can help survivors make sense of the narcissist's actions and detach from self-blame.

Narcissism in Society

Narcissism is not just an individual trait, it has woven itself into the fabric of modern society. From cultural norms that glorify self-promotion to the rise of technology that amplifies narcissistic tendencies, societal factors play a significant role in shaping, enabling, and even rewarding narcissistic behavior. Understanding how narcissism manifests at a societal level can provide deeper insights into its prevalence and impact.

The Role of Culture

Cultural values heavily influence the development and acceptance of narcissistic traits. In societies where individualism, success, and competition are prioritized, narcissistic behaviors are often encouraged and rewarded.

Individualism vs. Collectivism: Individualistic cultures place a high value on personal achievement and self-expression, which can foster self-centeredness. In contrast, collectivist cultures emphasize community and relationships, which may discourage overt narcissism.

Materialism and Success: The cultural obsession with wealth, status, and physical appearance creates an environment where narcissistic traits thrive. "Looking successful" often becomes more important than genuine achievement.

Influence of Media: Celebrities, influencers, and public figures who exhibit narcissistic behaviors are frequently idolized, reinforcing the idea that these traits lead to success.

The Impact of Social Media

The digital age has given narcissism a new stage to flourish. Social media platforms, designed to reward visibility and validation, have normalized behaviors associated with narcissistic traits.

Self-Promotion and Validation: Platforms like Instagram, TikTok, and Facebook encourage users to present idealized versions of their lives. The pursuit of likes, followers, and comments fuels the need for constant validation.

Comparison Culture: The curated lives of others create a cycle of comparison, fostering envy and insecurity. This, in turn, leads to more self-promotion as users try to compete for attention and admiration.

Trolling and Online Aggression: Narcissistic behaviors such as demeaning others, seeking dominance, or provoking reactions are amplified in the anonymity of online spaces.

Narcissism in Relationships

Society often normalizes or excuses toxic behaviors, making it harder for individuals to recognize narcissistic abuse in relationships.

Romantic Relationships: The idea of "toxic love" is glamorized in media, perpetuating unhealthy dynamics and emotional manipulation.

Workplace Narcissism: Narcissistic traits like dominance, confidence, and self-promotion are often mistaken for leadership qualities, allowing narcissistic individuals to thrive in corporate environments.

Narcissism and Consumerism

Modern consumer culture feeds narcissistic tendencies by associating self-worth with possessions, appearance, and social status.

Marketing and Advertising: Advertisers exploit insecurities, convincing consumers that they need certain products to feel worthy, attractive, or successful.

Luxury Culture: Owning expensive, branded items becomes a way to signal status and superiority, often fueling narcissistic competition.

The Consequences of a Narcissistic Society

The normalization of narcissism in society has far-reaching consequences:

Erosion of Empathy: As narcissistic traits become more prevalent, empathy and genuine connection are often sacrificed.

Increased Mental Health Issues: Constant comparison and validation-seeking behaviors contribute to anxiety, depression, and low self-esteem in individuals.

Weakening of Relationships: Narcissism fosters superficial connections, making it harder for people to form meaningful, lasting relationships.

Types of Narcissism

Narcissism is a spectrum, and not all narcissists exhibit the same behaviors or traits. Understanding the different types of narcissism can help survivors recognize the patterns they've experienced and make sense of their interactions with narcissistic individuals. Below are the most common types of narcissism:

Grandiose Narcissism

This is the classic image most people associate with narcissism. Grandiose narcissists are overtly confident, charming, and self-absorbed. They have an inflated sense of self-importance and crave admiration and validation from others. Their arrogance often masks deep insecurities, but they rarely acknowledge their vulnerabilities.

Traits:

- Exaggerated sense of superiority

- Need for constant attention and admiration

- Dismissive of others' feelings and needs

Vulnerable Narcissism

Unlike the grandiose type, vulnerable narcissists are hypersensitive and insecure. They often feel inadequate, resentful, or victimized. While they may not openly seek admiration, they have an underlying need for validation and tend to manipulate others through guilt or passive-aggressiveness.

Traits:
- Emotional fragility and hypersensitivity

- Passive-aggressive behavior

- Tendency to play the victim

Covert Narcissism

Covert narcissists are subtle in their approach, making their behavior harder to detect. They often appear humble or introverted but harbor a strong sense of entitlement and resentment. Their manipulation is less obvious, relying on guilt-tripping, backhanded compliments, or subtle put-downs. ***They are the most dangerous type of narcissists.***

Traits:
- Low outward confidence but high internal self-importance

- Passive manipulation and subtle arrogance

- Easily offended and prone to envy

Malignant Narcissism

This is another most dangerous type, as it combines narcissism with traits of antisocial personality disorder. Malignant narcissists lack empathy and remorse, often engaging in exploitative, manipulative, and even sadistic behavior. Their actions are driven by a desire for control and power, regardless of the harm they cause.

Traits:

- Aggressiveness and exploitation

- Lack of empathy or guilt

- Paranoia and a thirst for dominance

Communal Narcissism

Communal narcissists present themselves as altruistic and caring, often engaging in charitable or social causes. However, their actions are driven by a need for recognition and admiration rather than genuine concern for others. They thrive on the perception of being a "good person."

Traits:

- Preoccupation with appearing moral and generous

- Manipulates others by feigning empathy

- Seeks validation through community-oriented actions

Somatic Narcissism

Somatic narcissists focus on their physical appearance and body, deriving their self-worth from how they look. They are obsessed with maintaining an attractive appearance and often seek admiration for their physique, beauty, or sexual prowess.

Traits:

- Obsession with physical appearance and health

- Excessive focus on fitness, beauty, or sexual appeal

- Superficial relationships based on appearance

Cerebral Narcissism

Cerebral narcissists derive their self-worth from their intellect, knowledge, or perceived mental superiority. They often belittle others to feel smarter or more capable and use their intellect as a tool for control and manipulation.

Traits:

- Preoccupation with intellectual superiority

- Dismissive of others' ideas or contributions

- Uses knowledge as a weapon to demean others

Cycles of Abuse

The cycle of abuse in narcissistic relationships is a repetitive, manipulative pattern designed to gain control over the victim. It comprises three distinct stages—Idealization (Love-Bombing), Devaluation, and Discard. Each phase serves a purpose in breaking down the victim's autonomy, confidence, and sense of reality.

1. Idealization (Love-Bombing)

The cycle begins with an intense period of idealization, often called love-bombing. The narcissist presents themselves as the perfect partner, friend, or ally, showering the target with affection, attention, and praise. This stage is marked by grand gestures, flattery, and promises of a future so ideal that it seems almost too good to be true.

The purpose of this phase is to build trust and emotional dependence. Victims are drawn in by the narcissist's charm and feel seen, valued, and deeply connected. It's a strategic act of creating a pedestal for the victim to stand on, only to later pull it out from under them.

Common Tactics in the Idealization Phase:

- Over-the-top compliments and declarations of love.

- Acts of generosity or attentiveness that seem extraordinary.

- Highlighting how "special" the victim is compared to others.

- Creating a whirlwind romance or rapid bonding to deepen attachment.

2. Devaluation

Once the victim is emotionally invested, the narcissist shifts to the devaluation phase. The affection and admiration fade, replaced by criticism, neglect, and psychological manipulation. The narcissist begins to chip away at the victim's confidence, using subtle put-downs, blame-shifting, and gaslighting to make the victim feel inadequate and confused.

During this phase, the narcissist's true nature begins to emerge. They may alternate between coldness and intermittent affection, keeping the victim guessing and striving to regain the initial love-bombing attention. This inconsistency creates emotional dependency and keeps the victim trapped in the cycle.

Common Tactics in the Devaluation Phase:

- Criticizing the victim's appearance, intelligence, or behavior.

- Comparing the victim unfavorably to others.

- Dismissing or minimizing the victim's feelings and concerns.

- Using gaslighting to distort reality and make the victim question their sanity.

- Withholding affection, attention, or communication as a form of punishment.

3. Discard

In the final phase, the narcissist discards the victim, either emotionally or physically. This could involve abruptly ending the relationship, emotionally withdrawing, or treating the victim as though they no longer exist. The discard phase is the ultimate expression of the narcissist's lack of empathy and serves as a way to regain a sense of superiority.

In some cases, the discard is temporary—the narcissist may re-engage with the victim when it suits their needs, restarting the cycle. This is often referred to as hoovering, where the narcissist pulls the victim back into the relationship with promises of change or fleeting kindness.

Common Tactics in the Discard Phase:

- Abruptly ending the relationship without explanation.

- Ignoring or avoiding the victim entirely.

- Blaming the victim for the relationship's failure.

- Publicly smearing the victim's reputation to justify their behavior.

- Moving on to a new target while the victim is left to cope with the emotional devastation.

4. Hoovering

Hoovering is a term used to describe a manipulative tactic employed by narcissists to "suck" their victims back into a toxic relationship after a period of separation. The narcissist will often reach out with the intention of re-establishing control, making the victim feel guilty or emotionally obligated to return. Hoovering can take various forms, such as offering false promises, using emotional manipulation (like claiming they are suffering without you), or even threats of harm to make the victim feel responsible for their well-being.

The goal of hoovering is not reconciliation, but rather to regain the narcissist's emotional supply and to continue exerting control over the victim. It exploits the victim's emotions, such as guilt or concern for the narcissist, and can make it difficult to break free from the cycle of abuse. Recognizing hoovering and setting firm boundaries is crucial for those who have left narcissistic relationships.

Common Tactics in the Hoovering Phase:

Manipulative Promises of Change: The narcissist may offer empty promises of change, claiming that they've learned their lessons and will act differently if you return. These promises are often superficial and rarely followed through.

Excessive Attention and Flattery: They may flood you with excessive attention, compliments, and affection in an attempt to reignite the initial Connection, making you feel special and wanted again.

Playing the Victim Again: The narcissist may once again play the victim, telling you how miserable their life is without you, making you feel responsible for their happiness or well-being.

Guilt Tripping: They may use guilt tactics to make you feel as if you're abandoning them or causing their pain, despite their previous actions that led to the separation.

Promises of a Perfect Future: They might convince you that the problems of the past were misunderstandings or external circumstances and that, if you return, everything will be perfect this time around.

CHAPTER 4

Covert Narcissist and Traits: Wolf In Sheep's Clothing

"They are the epitome of a wolf in sheep's clothing"

I want to focus on covert narcissism because it leaves survivors in a deep state of confusion. Many struggle to recognize they were even in an abusive relationship because the abuse is disguised as "misunderstandings," "bad moods," or "just how they are." This makes it particularly dangerous. Covert narcissists destroy from within, and by the time you realize what's happening, the damage is already done. Understanding this type of narcissism is crucial because once you see it for what it is, you can begin to break free.

People often associate narcissism with loud, arrogant, and attention-seeking traits. However, some of the most dangerous narcissists don't fit this stereotype. They operate in the shadows, using subtle manipulation, victimhood, and quiet cruelty to break down their targets from the inside out. This is covert narcissism—one of the most damaging and hardest-to-recognize forms of narcissistic abuse.

Covert narcissists weaponize vulnerability. Unlike grandiose narcissists who flaunt superiority, covert narcissists adopt the persona of a misunderstood underdog. Using self-pity to gain control and extract sympathy. They paint themselves as victims, ensuring that any confrontation against them feels like an unwarranted attack.

Their manipulation is subtle. Instead of outright dismissing your ideas or achievements, they offer faint praise or backhanded compliments that leave you doubting yourself. These comments chip away at your confidence while maintaining an outward appearance of kindness.

Covert narcissists don't just manipulate they make you their blueprint. Every insecurity, past wound, and trauma you've shared with them becomes ammunition in their psychological warfare. They store and strategically use this information to break you down, dismantle your support system, and isolate you from those who might help you see the truth.

What makes covert narcissists particularly dangerous is their ability to **mirror empathy**. They excel at identifying emotions, but instead of connecting with you, they use this skill to manipulate. They feign understanding and support in moments of vulnerability, only to later use your secrets against you in a subtle but cutting way.

Covert narcissists create confusion in relationships. They thrive on indirect communication and ambiguity, leaving you constantly second-guessing their intentions. This strategy is known as cognitive dissonance, keeps you emotionally unsteady and dependent on their approval.

Perhaps the most devastating impact of a covert narcissist is the deep sense of isolation they create. By undermining your confidence and alienating you from others, they ensure you become reliant on them for validation. Over time you feel like you've lost your sense of self, constantly walking on eggshells and doubting your own reality.

At first, they seem like the perfect confidant, listening intently and offering validation for your pain. But over time, they twist your trauma against you. If you fear abandonment, they play on that fear—subtly making you feel that no one else cares for you like they do. If you struggle with self-doubt, they reinforce it, making you question your instincts and judgment. They strike exactly where it destabilizes you the most.

One of their most dangerous tactics is turning your loved ones against you. They do this carefully, never outright attacking but planting seeds of doubt and manipulation. They might tell your friends or family that they're "worried about you" or that you've "been acting differently." To you, they'll say things like, "I don't think your best friend has your best interests at heart" or "Your family never really supports you, have you noticed?" Over time, this erodes your trust in those around you, making it easier for the narcissist to isolate you.

This slow destruction of your support system ensures that when they escalate their manipulation, you have nowhere to turn. They make sure you're emotionally exhausted, confused, and dependent on them. And just when you start to regain your strength, they use the very trauma they once pretended to help you heal from to humiliate, guilt-trip, and reinforce your worst fears.

Covert narcissists don't just live in their own delusions—they actively manifest them into reality. Their minds are wired for paranoia, fear, and control. Instead of processing their insecurities rationally, they project them onto others. But projection alone isn't enough. They need validation that their fears are justified, so they create situations to prove themselves right, even if it means destroying relationships, fabricating crises, or driving their victims into emotional distress.

It starts with a fabricated belief—an unfounded fear that exists solely in their minds. Maybe they believe you will betray, abandon, or outshine them as they fear exposure, rejection, or replacement. Instead of questioning whether these fears are rational. They manipulate the environment to make them come true. If they suspect you will leave them, they'll push you away with passive-aggressive behavior, silent treatment, or sudden emotional withdrawal, forcing you into frustration and self-doubt. The moment you react or pull away, they use your response as proof—"See? You were going to leave me all along."

The worst part? They truly believe their own lies. In their mind, they aren't the manipulators– they are the victims of a cruel world that constantly betrays them. But in reality, they are the architects of their own suffering, using deceit, paranoia, and emotional sabotage to turn their delusions into truth. If you're in their path, you become nothing more than a pawn in their twisted game, caught in a cycle of blame, gaslighting, and chaos.

> *"These narcissists should come with a warning label. Because of their humble, empathetic, vulnerable demeanor, they can appear the opposite of their grandiose counter part and much more difficult to detect. Their abuse is insidious, coercive and can be extremely difficult to spot. The passive aggressive way they convey their deceitful nature, makes it confusing for victims to understand if their intentions are truly bad or just misunderstood. And that is exactly the way they want it. It is a cowards way to abuse people and deny their true motives. They tend to primarily abuse their loved ones or anyone who they are closely involved with. To the outside world they appear like the nicest people in the world."*

How To Identify A Covert Narcissist?

Identifying the covert narcissist can be challenging because they disguise their grandiosity behind a facade of humility and victimhood. If you find yourself constantly second guessing your words and walking on egg shells—Its important to be aware of the covert narcissist traits:

Lack of Empathy:
Despite appearing sensitive or shy, covert narcissists struggle to genuinely empathize with others. They may appear caring, but their actions often reveal a lack of concern for anyone else's feelings or needs.

Fragile Self-Esteem:
Covert narcissists have deep-seated insecurities and low self-esteem. They are highly sensitive to criticism and may feel wounded even by mild feedback.

Grandiosity (but Secretive):
While they don't openly display their superiority, covert narcissists maintain a secret sense of grandiosity. They believe they are special or more deserving than others but mask it with self-deprecation or quiet disdain.

Passive-Aggressiveness:
Rather than openly confront others, covert narcissists express their anger or frustration through passive-aggressive behaviors, like giving the silent treatment, withholding affection, or making sarcastic remarks.

Victim Mentality:
Covert narcissists often position themselves as victims, playing on others' sympathies. They frequently complain about how others mistreat or misunderstand them, deflecting attention from their own faults.

Isolating a Partner:
They subtly manipulate and control their partner by isolating them from friends or family. This ensures their partner is dependent on them for emotional support, making it easier to manipulate.

Need for Admiration:
Though they crave admiration like overt narcissists, covert narcissists tend to seek it in a roundabout way. They might fish for compliments or use self-pity to get validation, rather than boasting outright.

Emotional Manipulation:
Covert narcissists often manipulate others emotionally, guilt-tripping or gaslighting their partner to maintain control and superiority.

Envy and Resentment:
These individuals feel envious of others' success or happiness. This envy may manifest in undermining comments or resentment, though they rarely express these feelings directly.

Social Withdrawal:
They avoid social situations where they risk not being the center of attention or might feel undervalued. This withdrawal can make them appear introverted, but it's often driven by their fear of not being admired.

Self-Absorption:
Even though they seem humble or quiet, covert narcissists are still deeply self-centered, focusing primarily on their own needs and feelings while minimizing others.

Strange Habits of Narcissists

Many of us are familiar with the narcissistic personality's classic traits such as grandiosity, rage and lack of empathy, but there are other things narcissists do often mistaken for individual personality quirks that are actually explainable aspects of pathological narcissism.

1. **They bend over backward to help others but ignore their own family**
   A narcissist may go out of their way to appear generous and helpful to outsiders, often doing grand gestures for acquaintances, colleagues, or even strangers. However, at home, they completely neglect their own family's needs, treating their loved ones with cold indifference or even hostility. This is because they seek admiration and validation from others and wants to maintain a good image to the outside world, while those closest to them already see through their facade.

2. **They act weird when you're sick and indifferent and cold to your pain**
   If you're feeling unwell, a narcissist may respond with complete indifference or even irritation rather than concern. Instead of caring for you, they might become distant, make insensitive remarks, or even seem annoyed that you're not able to cater to their needs. Sometimes, they might feign concern in front of others but show zero empathy when alone with you.

3. **They always walk ahead of you**
   Whether you're walking down the street, in a mall, or even at a family event, a narcissist will often walk ahead, making no effort to match your pace. This is a power move—subtly signaling that they are superior, more

important, and in control. Walking ahead also reinforces their lack of emotional connection, as they don't consider you an equal partner.

4. **Random accusations out of nowhere**
Out of the blue, they will accuse you of things you haven't done—cheating, lying, manipulating them, or having bad intentions. These accusations often come as projections of their own behaviors, meaning they might actually be the ones engaging in such actions. Accusations also serve as a way to destabilize you emotionally, keeping you in a defensive and confused state. *"Narcissist's accusations are confessions"*

5. **Oversleeping or staying in bed all day**
Some narcissists will oversleep excessively, using it as a way to escape responsibilities or gain attention. They might act exhausted as if life is too difficult, expecting others to cater to them while they do nothing. This behavior can also be a form of passive-aggressive control—if they sleep in, others have to pick up the slack.

6. **Sending excessively long messages out of nowhere**
A narcissist might go silent for days and then suddenly send you an overwhelming, essay-like message, packed with complaints, emotional manipulation, or attempts to reestablish control. These messages may shift blame onto you, guilt-trip you, or create drama just when you thought they were finally out of your life.

7. **Mocking you in front of family and friends**
They deliberately mock you in front of family and friends to humiliate and belittle you, stripping away your confidence while maintaining their charming facade. Whether through sarcastic jokes, imitating you, or exposing your insecurities, their goal is to degrade you under the guise of humor. If you call them out, they'll dismiss your feelings by saying, "You're too sensitive" or "It was just a joke," ensuring they avoid accountability while chipping away at your self-worth.

8. **They traumatize you before your important events**

   No matter the occasion—whether you're graduating, auditioning, or celebrating your birthday—they find a way to make it about them and sabotage your moment. Out of nowhere, they create a tense, hostile environment through silent treatment, indifference, or unnecessary arguments. Their goal is to make you feel guilty for having a special day, ensuring you can never fully enjoy it or experience true happiness.

9. **Hypocrisy**

   NARCISSISTS are such hypocrites. They pretend to have morals, standards, feelings and a conscience but they possess none of these. They will lie, insult, cheat, abuse and disrespect you, but in return they will expect fidelity, respect and all your time and energy spent on them. They can do whatever they want, whenever they want, but you are to remain loyal and perfect at all times. This isn't healthy—it's toxic and definitely not love.

10. **No eye contact with you while talking**

    When speaking to you, a narcissist deliberately avoid eye contact. They do this as a form of control, disinterest, or even contempt. By avoiding eye contact, they make you feel like *you* are beneath them and they disgust you and aren't worth acknowledging. This subtle act can leave you feeling invisible, unimportant, or devalued. However, when they are in a fit of rage, their pupils are often dilated, revealing the intensity of their hatred and rage almost looking demonic. In moments of manipulation or intimidation, they may switch to intense, piercing eye contact, making you feel trapped under their scrutiny.

11. **They value the opinions of strangers over family**

    They will make you feel insignificant by constantly dismissing your ideas, questioning your intelligence, and acting as if your input holds no value. No matter how well-informed or experienced you are, they will find a way to undermine you—whether through condescending remarks, outright rejection, or passive-aggressive indifference. Yet, paradoxically, they will eagerly embrace advice from an outsider, whether it's a random acquaintance, a so-called expert, or even an influencer on social media. They crave external validation and assume that others must know better than you, not because it's true, but because devaluing you reinforces their sense of superiority.

12. **Strange relationship with sex**
Covert narcissists have a complex and manipulative approach to sex, using it either as a tool for control or indulging in it excessively to feed their ego. When used for control, they withhold intimacy to punish, manipulate, or make their partner feel unwanted, conditioning them to seek approval and comply with their demands.

13. **Making Up Funny Stories to Impress Others**
Narcissists have a habit of inventing exaggerated or completely false stories; especially funny or dramatic encounters with strangers to make themselves seem interesting, likable, or admired. They might claim a random stranger praised them, had an unforgettable interaction with them, or that they handled a situation in a way that made everyone laugh. These stories are often told with great confidence and detail, making them seem believable, but if you were actually there, you'd know it never happened. They do this to manufacture charm, gain attention, and create an illusion of being more charismatic or influential than they really are.

14. **Create Urgency**
Narcissists manipulate through urgency by creating a false sense of pressure, forcing their victims to react without thinking critically. They manufacture crises, demand immediate decisions, and use time-sensitive ultimatums to keep you off balance and compliant. Whether it's rushing a relationship, pressuring you into financial commitments, or provoking emotional reactions, they thrive on making you feel like you have no time to assess the situation rationally. The faster you react, the easier you are to control.

Narcissists and Addictions

Narcissists often struggle with various forms of addiction, which serve as a means to escape their inner feelings of inadequacy, boredom, or emotional emptiness. These addictions can become tools they use to either fuel their sense of superiority or to cope with their inability to regulate emotions effectively. Let's break down some of these common addictions and how they manifest in narcissistic behavior:

1. **Gaming Addiction**
    Narcissists addicted to gaming may use video games as an escape from real-life responsibilities or relationships. The gaming world gives them a sense of control, power, and recognition—things they constantly crave. Online gaming, in particular, may become a platform for them to dominate, manipulate, or display superiority over others, fulfilling their need for attention and admiration.

2. **Substance Abuse (Drugs and Smoking)**
    Many narcissists turn to substances like drugs or alcohol to numb feelings of vulnerability, shame, or inadequacy. Substance abuse allows them to avoid confronting their internal struggles, and they may also use it as a means to seek attention or sympathy. When intoxicated, their behaviors often become more erratic and abusive, magnifying their manipulative tendencies and lack of accountability.

3. **Alcohol Addiction**
    Alcohol can serve as a coping mechanism for narcissists, helping them mask their insecurities or amplify their grandiose self-image. They may use drinking as a way to loosen up in social situations, seek attention by being the "life of the party," or justify destructive behavior. When drunk, their emotional instability and manipulative tendencies often intensify, leading to explosive outbursts or harmful actions.

4. **Prostitution or Sex Addiction**

    Some narcissists develop an addiction to sex or engage in frequent use of prostitutes to validate their sense of power and desirability. They often seek the thrill of conquest or the illusion of control in these encounters, which temporarily feeds their ego. This addiction can stem from their inability to form deep, meaningful connections and their constant need for external validation. On the other hand, some covert narcissists become consumed by their own desires, often developing compulsive behaviors like porn addiction or seeking indulgence with prostitutes as an extension of their deep-seated misogyny. Their objectification of women and lack of emotional connection drive them toward transactional encounters, where they can assert dominance without accountability. In male covert narcissists, this addiction and detachment from real intimacy can lead to erectile dysfunction, as their reliance on artificial stimulation and dehumanizing views of women further distort their ability to form genuine connections, reinforcing cycles of frustration and emotional neglect.

5. **Addiction to Control and Power**

    Beyond physical addictions, narcissists are also addicted to control and power in relationships and situations. This addiction drives them to manipulate others, dominate conversations, and exert influence in all areas of their life. The high they get from controlling others mirrors the satisfaction others might get from substances or gambling.

Psychology behind Addictions

- **Escaping Vulnerability**: Addictions provide narcissists with an easy way to avoid facing their deeper insecurities or vulnerabilities. Rather than dealing with their inner emotional struggles, they rely on addictive behaviors to suppress them.

- **Feeding Their Ego**: Many of their addictions (like sex, alcohol, or gaming) feed their ego by making them feel more powerful, admired, or in control.

- **Lack of Accountability**: Narcissists rarely take responsibility for their actions. Addiction allows them to create excuses for their behavior, shifting blame to others or external circumstances.

How These Addictions Affect Others

The narcissist's addictive behaviors can wreak havoc on their relationships. They prioritize their addictions over the needs of their partner and children, creating instability and emotional distress for those around them. Their addictions can also amplify their abusive tendencies, making them more unpredictable, manipulative, and selfish.

Recognizing these patterns is crucial for survivors in relationships with narcissists. Understanding their addictive tendencies helps survivors set boundaries, disengage, and protect themselves from the destructive cycles that addictions perpetuate.

A Cheating Narcissist

Narcissists lead secretive lives—**they are cheaters**. They will always cheat on you, always have affairs behind your back, and they are exceptionally skilled at hiding their double life. You may never realize how long they've been unfaithful, or perhaps by the end of the relationship, you uncover a web of lies that had been there all along. Their ability to compartmentalize, deceive, and manipulate ensures their affairs remain **undetected** for years.

If they are caught cheating and confronted, their reaction is a whirlwind of deflection, denial, and manipulation. Rather than owning up to their betrayal, they twist the narrative into a performance of victimhood or outright rage. They may accuse you of being insecure, paranoid, or even blame you for their infidelity—claiming you were neglectful, unloving, or not "good enough." They gaslight you into questioning your own reality, making you doubt the very evidence in front of you. If denial doesn't work, they resort to rage—shouting, attacking, or even smearing you to others to maintain their image.

No matter how much proof you have, they will never give you closure. A narcissist's cheating isn't just about physical betrayal—it's about control, emotional torment, and the thrill of getting away with it.

Narcissist and Dead Eyes

One of the most unsettling experiences in dealing with a narcissist is witnessing their "dead eyes"—a lifeless, hollow gaze that seems to strip away any sense of humanity. It's a look that can shift and morph depending on the situation, but at its core, it reflects the emotional emptiness inside them.

How Their Eyes Change in Different Situations

1. **The Predatory Stare**
   This intense, unblinking gaze is often seen during love bombing or manipulation. It's the look of someone who is studying you, assessing your weaknesses, and figuring out how to gain control. It feels invasive, like they're looking *through* you rather than *at* you.

2. **The Glazed-Over Look**
   When confronted with real emotions—especially those they don't want to deal with—narcissists can suddenly seem vacant. Their eyes become dull, as if they're mentally elsewhere. This happens when a victim expresses pain, sadness, or tries to hold them accountable. Instead of engaging, they detach, showing complete indifference.

3. **The Rage Eyes**
   Perhaps the most terrifying of all, this happens when they feel challenged, exposed, or powerless. Their pupils dilate, their expression darkens, and their entire demeanor shifts into something almost inhuman. It's the look of someone who is no longer pretending to be in control—it's raw, explosive anger bubbling to the surface. Many survivors describe this moment as feeling like they were staring into the eyes of a monster.

4. **The Flat, Expressionless Stare**
   This is common when they are discarding someone or when they no longer see value in a person. Their face goes blank, their eyes turn cold, and there's a complete emotional detachment. It's as if they've erased your existence in real time. No remorse, no care—just emptiness.

Why Their Eyes Look Dead? Narcissists lack genuine emotional depth. They mimic emotions but don't truly feel them the way empathetic people do. Their eyes betray their internal void—there's no warmth, no real connection, just a hollow existence driven by control, validation, and power.

Many survivors recall a moment when they TRULY saw the narcissist for what they were, often during a rage episode or a discard. When the mask slipped, and their eyes reflected exactly what was inside—NOTHING.

Weaponize the Legal System

Narcissists do not see the legal system as a means of justice—they see it as another tool for control, intimidation, and revenge. They exploit every loophole available, manipulate authorities, and use the system against their victims in the most malicious ways possible. Understanding their tactics and knowing how to counteract them is essential for surviving legal battles with a narcissist.

1. **How Narcissists Manipulate Courts, Police, and Child Protection Services**

    o   **False allegations:** They file baseless claims of domestic abuse, neglect, or parental alienation, child abuse to turn authorities against you.

    o   **Playing the victim:** They present themselves as the caring, stable parent or spouse while painting you as irrational, unstable, or even dangerous.

    o   **Deliberate delays:** Narcissists often file unnecessary motions, refuse to cooperate, and prolong court proceedings to drain your financial and emotional resources.

    o   **Manipulating child protective services:** They may report false claims of child endangerment or neglect to gain leverage in custody battles.

    o   **Harassment through legal channels:** They repeatedly file baseless lawsuits or emergency hearings just to keep you in constant legal turmoil.

2. **Legal Loopholes Narcissists Exploit**

    o   **Dragging out divorce proceedings** to avoid asset division and maintain financial control.

    o   **Hiding assets** through family members, offshore accounts, or undisclosed income.

    o   **Exploiting the 'friendly parent' rule** by pretending to encourage co-parenting while sabotaging your custody rights.

    o   **Filing for sole custody** to punish you, even if they have no real interest in parenting.

    o   **Weaponizing restraining orders** by falsely accusing you of harassment to cut you off from children or shared resources.

Are Narcissists Psychopaths?

Many people mistakenly believe that narcissists and psychopaths are entirely different, but the truth is far more disturbing. While there are key differences, narcissists **do** have psychopathy embedded in their behavior. The deception, manipulation, and cruelty they inflict on others are not just traits of narcissism—they also mirror psychopathy.

Sociopaths and Narcissistic Personality Disorder are both personality disorders that form when the person is under the age of **seven**. Unfortunately, there is no going back and reforming a sociopaths' personality formation or structure. Likewise, narcissism cannot be reversed either.

I am talking to the people who have experienced first hand a level of narcissism that almost cost them their life. A narcissism overlayed with a level of psychopathy and type of darkness that may still be hard to grapple and come to terms with because it is so **insidious** in nature, and done so directly to them with so much **pristine calculation**, while hiding behind and wearing a mask of charm, confidence and friendliness to those around them.

Pathological Liars:

Narcissists don't just lie to others; they lie to themselves. Their entire identity is built on **delusion**—a carefully constructed false reality where they are superior, blameless, and entitled to control others. They don't perceive reality as it is—instead, they twist it to fit their grandiose self-image. When confronted with the truth, they **double down on their false narratives rather than accept responsibility**. This is where **psychopathy, sociopathy, pathological lying, and delusion** all collide—creating a person who not only deceives others but also convinces themselves that their deception is the truth.

Sociopaths:

A narcissistic sociopath does not experience genuine empathy, but they are masters at faking it when necessary. They can charm, lie, and manipulate their way into positions of power, making people believe they are kind, caring, or even self-sacrificing. However, behind closed doors, they are ruthless, cruel, and indifferent to the pain they inflict. Unlike a standard narcissist who thrives on admiration, a narcissistic sociopath thrives on dominance— getting pleasure not just from being praised but from seeing others suffer under their control. They engage in deceit, fraud, and emotional abuse without hesitation, feeling no guilt for the destruction they cause. **They lack a moral compass, acting purely on self-interest, regardless of who gets hurt in the process.**

Jordan Peterson once said, ***"If you think tough men are dangerous, wait until you see what weak men are capable of."*** A narcissistic sociopath embodies this statement completely. Their outward confidence and arrogance mask a deep-seated insecurity that makes them unable to handle rejection or failure.

Psychopath:

Narcissists and psychopaths share strikingly similar traits, often blurring the lines between the two. Both lack empathy, using others as tools for their personal gain without any regard for their feelings or well-being. A narcissist manipulates to maintain their inflated self-image, while a psychopath manipulates to gain power and control, often without any emotional investment in the outcome. Both are expert liars, twisting the truth to suit their needs and create a reality where they are always the victim or the superior one.

"Psychopathy is a personality disorder characterized by an inability to feel remorse, guilt, or empathy, and an unrelenting drive to manipulate others for personal gain. It's a profound distortion of the self that leaves destruction in its wake." - Jordan Peterson

CHAPTER 5

ENABLERS AND FLYING MONKEYS

Enablers and flying monkeys play a crucial role in the perpetuation of a narcissist's abuse, often unknowingly or out of their own psychological motivations. While narcissists are the ones actively causing harm, enablers and flying monkeys serve as facilitators, allowing the abusive cycle to continue unchecked. Enablers, typically individuals close to the narcissist, actively or passively support the narcissist's behavior, either out of fear, a desire for approval, or because they don't understand the full scope of the narcissist's manipulations. These individuals might downplay the severity of the narcissist's actions, dismissing the victim's concerns or even gaslighting the victim by reinforcing the narcissist's distorted version of reality. In doing so, enablers become complicit in the abuse, aiding in the narcissist's control over the victim and perpetuating their manipulation.

Flying monkeys, on the other hand, are individuals who have been recruited or manipulated by the narcissist to further isolate and discredit the victim. The narcissist uses these people as pawns to spread lies, create division, and enact emotional abuse on their behalf. Flying monkeys are often unaware of the harm they're causing, believing they are helping the narcissist or taking the narcissist's side out of loyalty, guilt or confusion. The narcissist often plays the victim, portraying themselves as misunderstood or wronged, thus manipulating the flying monkeys into attacking the real victim on their behalf. These individuals are typically guilt-tripped or brainwashed into believing the narcissist's false narrative.

While enablers and flying monkeys may not engage in direct abuse, their actions can be just as damaging, especially in the victim's emotional and mental state. Enablers validate the narcissist's toxic behavior, normalizing the abuse and making it harder for the victim to stand up for themselves. They also encourage the victim to ignore or suppress their feelings, undermining their sense of reality and reinforcing the narcissist's power. Flying monkeys, on the other hand, exacerbate the victim's isolation by spreading lies and rumors, further confusing the victim and causing them to question their worth or their perception of events. Both groups create an environment where the narcissist's abuse is excused, supported, and protected, often trapping the victim in a cycle of confusion and shame.

It's important to note that enablers and flying monkeys may not be fully aware of the harm they are causing. However, this does not absolve them of responsibility. By continuing to support the narcissist or participating in the gaslighting, manipulation, and smear campaigns, they become active participants in the abuse. Their actions can have long-lasting effects on the victim's mental health, reinforcing feelings of guilt, self-doubt and emotional instability. In some cases, these individuals may even play a more damaging role than the narcissist, because their involvement often creates confusion and makes it harder for the victim to escape or seek support.

Recognizing the role of enablers and flying monkeys is critical in understanding the full extent of narcissistic abuse. While the narcissist is the primary source of harm, those who support, defend, or assist in the abuse are equally responsible for the emotional and psychological damage inflicted on the victim. For a victim to heal, it is important to not only recognize the narcissist's manipulations but also the role of these secondary abusers in maintaining the cycle of abuse.

Mother-In-Law The Biggest Enabler

In a narcissistic family cult, the dynamics operate like an unspoken hierarchy, with the narcissist ruling at the center and the enablers orbiting them, feeding their power. A narcissistic mother-in-law plays the role of a self-appointed matriarch, dictating the terms of everyone's existence under her shadow. She thrives on control, demands loyalty, and fosters an environment where the family revolves around her and the narcissist's needs, at the expense of anyone who dares to disrupt the fragile structure. For the victim—often the daughter-in-law, this dynamic becomes a living nightmare as the narcissistic mother-in-law (MIL) enables her son's abuse while actively contributing her own.

This MIL wears a facade of warmth and authority to the outside world, presenting herself as the glue that holds the family together. Behind closed doors, however, she wields her power ruthlessly, using manipulation and emotional blackmail to keep everyone in line. She takes pride in her son's narcissistic traits, viewing him as an extension of herself—a golden child who can do no wrong. His abusive tendencies are not just excused but often encouraged. To the MIL, the victim's suffering is not an unfortunate consequence but a necessary byproduct of maintaining her family's twisted order. By supporting her son's abuse, she protects her own sense of superiority and ensures her position of control remains unchallenged.

The MIL's support of the narcissist is not passive—it's deeply calculated. She may actively contribute to the victim's humiliation, chipping away at their self-esteem through subtle digs or overt criticism. If the victim ever tries to stand up to the narcissist, the MIL is the first to leap to his defense, framing the victim as ungrateful or difficult. She thrives on division, using triangulation to pit family members against each other and isolating the victim from potential allies. "We're family, and family stays together," she'll declare, but her definition of family only serves to perpetuate control and oppression.

The narcissistic MIL benefits immensely from this arrangement. By enabling her son's abusive behavior, she keeps him tethered to her, ensuring her role in his life remains indispensable. She depends on him financially, emotionally, or socially and she sees the victim as a threat to this bond. To neutralize this threat, she works to dismantle the victim's confidence and independence, subtly encouraging the narcissist to exert more control. In some cases, she becomes an active participant in financial abuse, hoarding resources or dictating how money is spent within the family, leaving the victim disempowered and dependent.

What makes the MIL particularly dangerous is her ability to blend manipulation with a veneer of maternal concern. She might portray herself as the "peacekeeper," someone who only wants the best for the family, while simultaneously gaslighting the victim into questioning their reality. If the victim tries to speak out or seek support, the MIL flips the narrative, painting herself and her son as the real victims of the victim's "unreasonable" behavior. This ensures that the victim is further alienated and left doubting their own perception.

The abuse doesn't stop at emotional or psychological manipulation—it extends to undermining the victim's relationship with their children, if there are any. The MIL might subtly sabotage the victim's parenting, encouraging the narcissist to counter-parent or alienate the children from their mother. She may plant seeds of doubt in the children's minds, making them question their mother's decisions or painting her as unstable. This ensures that the MIL's influence over the next generation remains strong, securing her legacy of control.

For the victim, living under the shadow of a narcissistic MIL and her golden child is a relentless cycle of invalidation and abuse. It's not just about surviving the narcissist's tactics—it's about navigating the web of enablers who uphold and amplify his behavior. The MIL's loyalty to her son, at the expense of the victim's humanity, makes her a central figure in the victim's suffering. Her complicity, whether through overt actions or silent approval, ensures that the narcissistic abuse thrives and deepens.

Breaking free from such a toxic family dynamic requires more than leaving the narcissist—it involves untangling oneself from the entire cult-like system that supports him, including the MIL who acts as his most devoted ally.

"In a narcissistic family cult, the mother-in-law isn't just an enabler—she's the mastermind." She's the architect of her son's narcissistic tendencies, having groomed him from childhood to reflect her own manipulative ways and to prioritize her above all else. She has taught him the very tactics he uses to control and abuse his wife, molding him into an extension of herself. Her influence doesn't end when he marries—in fact, it intensifies as she works tirelessly to maintain her grip over him, ensuring no outside love or attachment can threaten her position. She sees her daughter-in-law as competition, not as family, and will go to great lengths to sabotage the relationship under the guise of maternal concern.

This mother-in-law is a master manipulator, capable of twisting any situation to fit the narrative that suits her. She can take a minor disagreement and inflate it into an argument that paints her as the victim and the daughter-in-law as the villain. She thrives on creating chaos, knowing that confusion and division keep her in control. Her insecurity drives her every move—she fears losing her son's attention, respect, and financial support, so she carefully orchestrates every aspect of his life to ensure he remains tethered to her. Her insecurity is her fuel, and she uses it to manipulate him into believing that she is the only person who truly cares for him, the only one who knows what's best.

Financially, she reaps immense benefits from this dynamic. Her son spends more on her than on his own children, prioritizing her desires above his responsibilities as a husband and father. She ensures this by inserting herself into every financial decision he makes. Whether it's buying furniture, choosing gifts or even determining if his wife deserves a shopping trip; she has the final say. She decides how the household is run, what the wife should or shouldn't wear, and even how he should treat his child. It's as if she's living her son's life by proxy, dictating every move he makes. The wife and children are left sidelined, their needs overlooked, as the narcissistic MIL enjoys the fruits of her control.

Her son, the narcissist, is deeply entrenched in this toxic relationship with his mother. He runs to her for advice on everything, no matter how trivial or personal. Yet, he is not entirely truthful with her. Behind her back, he lives a separate life, one she isn't privy to. This duality allows him to maintain a facade of loyalty while indulging in his own selfish desires. But this dishonesty doesn't bother her as much as the thought of losing her influence over him. She turns a blind eye to his deceit, as long as her position as the central figure in his life remains unchallenged.

For the victim—the daughter-in-law, this dynamic is suffocating. It's not just about enduring the abuse from her husband—it's about battling the constant interference and manipulation of a MIL who views her as nothing more than an obstacle to be removed. The MIL's insecurities manifest in her obsessive need to control her son's life, and by extension, his wife's life too. The victim is subjected to a relentless power struggle, where her autonomy, her choices, and even her identity are under siege. She is left questioning her worth as she watches her husband prioritize his mother's whims over the well-being of their family.

This narcissistic MIL is the puppet master, pulling the strings of everyone in her family cult. Her son is her most **loyal puppet**, trained to carry out her will while feeding her ego and bank account. But her control comes at a cost; the destruction of relationships, the erosion of trust, and the emotional devastation of the victim. Breaking free from such a toxic system is not just about escaping the narcissist; it's about breaking the entire cycle of manipulation that the MIL has carefully crafted.

Male Narcissists and Mother Wound

Many male narcissists grow up with mothers who are excessively controlling and emotionally suffocating. In many cases, these mothers have experienced mistreatment at the hands of their own partners and as a result, shift their emotional needs onto their sons. Instead of providing the child with a nurturing, balanced environment, the mother treats him as her emotional crutch, expecting him to fulfill the void left by her own dysfunctional relationship. This dynamic causes the child to develop an inflated sense of self-importance, feeling simultaneously powerful yet trapped under his mother's influence. Even as he grows into adulthood, he remains emotionally enmeshed with her, unable to establish true independence. This often leaves him feeling emasculated, but instead of confronting his mother's control, he redirects his unresolved frustration and emotional imbalance onto his romantic partners.

One way he enacts this subconscious revenge is through relentless criticism. Just as his mother may have judged, nitpicked, or made him feel inadequate growing up, he projects the same behavior onto his partner. No matter what she does, it is never good enough. He fixates on the smallest details, undermining her confidence and ensuring she feels the same sense of unworthiness that he once experienced. His words are designed to break her down so that she, too, questions her self-worth, just as he did under his mother's scrutiny.

Playing the victim is another deeply ingrained response. Growing up, he may have internalized the belief that he was responsible for his mother's struggles, constantly being blamed for her unhappiness. Rather than acknowledging the toxicity of that dynamic, he unconsciously recreates it in his relationships. Every issue, no matter how trivial, becomes her fault. He deflects responsibility for his actions and manipulates situations to make her feel like she is the source of his misery, just as his mother made him feel. By doing so, he regains a twisted sense of control, ensuring that his partner carries the same burden of blame that he once bore.

Control itself becomes a primary need for him, driven by his childhood experience of powerlessness. As a child, he had no control over his mother's emotions, demands, or expectations. Now, as an adult, he compensates for that lack of control by exerting dominance over his partner. He dictates decisions, enforces rules, and ensures that his will is followed without question. His desire to control every aspect of the relationship stems from an unconscious need to reclaim what was denied to him as a child—autonomy, authority, and emotional stability.

Loyalty tests are another weapon he wields, replaying his deep-seated fears of abandonment. If he felt neglected, used, or emotionally let down by his mother, he carries that wound into his romantic relationships. He creates situations that force his partner to prove her loyalty, often by accusing her of betrayal or infidelity without any basis. He pushes her to her limits, manufacturing emotional crises just to see if she will stay, much like a wounded child testing whether his mother will abandon him or continue to soothe his insecurities. However, these tests are designed to be impossible to pass—no amount of reassurance ever truly satisfies his need for security because he is still chasing the validation his mother never gave him.

Ultimately, his greatest weapon is psychological and emotional destruction. He systematically breaks his partner down through mental, verbal, and emotional abuse. His goal is to strip away her strength, making her dependent on him just as he was once emotionally dependent on his mother. He uses manipulation, gaslighting, and demeaning remarks to ensure she feels weak, lost, and uncertain of her own reality. The more broken she becomes, the more power he feels–power that he never had under his mother's control but now craves in his relationships.

This entire cycle of destruction is not always consciously planned, but it is deeply ingrained in his psyche. The unresolved wounds from his childhood become the foundation of his abusive tendencies. Without self-awareness and true emotional healing he remains trapped in this pattern, using every relationship as a battleground to reenact his past trauma, making his partner the new recipient of his mother's vengeance.

Delusion is the culprit

A male narcissist who has been emotionally enmeshed with his mother rarely, if ever, sees her as the true source of his pain. Instead, he remains deeply loyal to her, trapped in a psychological illusion where she is the ultimate figure of love, sacrifice, and righteousness. This distorted perception prevents him from acknowledging the damage she inflicted, because doing so would mean confronting the painful reality that the very person who was supposed to nurture and protect him was, in fact, the one who wounded him the most.

From a young age, he was conditioned to believe that his mother's needs, emotions, and struggles took precedence over his own. She may have played the role of the martyr—suffering at the hands of an abusive or absent father and in doing so, she ingrained in him the belief that she was the victim, not the perpetrator. He learned that his role was to protect, support, and cater to her, often at the cost of his own emotional well-being. This dynamic prevents him from ever questioning her behavior, as he has been programmed to see her as a saint rather than as a controlling or abusive figure.

To acknowledge that his mother was the source of his pain would mean admitting that his entire emotional foundation is flawed. It would require him to face the unbearable truth that he was never truly loved for who he was, but rather for the role he played in her life. This realization is too threatening, as it would shatter the very identity he has constructed—one where he is either the dutiful son or the misunderstood victim of cruel women who fail to appreciate him. Instead of confronting the toxic maternal influence that shaped him, he transfers his resentment onto his romantic partners, finding in them an easier, more accessible target.

When he criticizes, blames, and controls his partner, he is unconsciously reenacting the relationship dynamic he experienced with his mother. However, rather than seeing himself as the victim in that relationship, he assumes the role of the aggressor, reversing the power imbalance he once felt as a child. By making his partner suffer, he unknowingly seeks revenge for the emotional suffocation and control he endured—except he directs it at the wrong person. His mother escapes blame entirely, while his partner is cast as the villain.

Even when confronted with evidence of his mother's manipulative nature, he is likely to defend her, making excuses for her behavior. He might say, **"She did the best she could,"** or, **"She had a hard life,"** rationalizing the abuse in a way that keeps him from facing the truth. His cognitive dissonance runs so deep that even in adulthood, he may continue to seek her validation, craving her approval while simultaneously resenting the hold she has over him. Any attempt to hold her accountable would be met with overwhelming guilt, as she has likely instilled in him the belief that questioning her equals betrayal.

This inability to recognize his mother's role as the true source of his trauma keeps him in a perpetual cycle of dysfunctional relationships. Each time he feels emasculated, abandoned, or disrespected by a partner, he reacts not just to the current situation but to years of unresolved childhood wounds. Instead of recognizing that his pain originates from his mother's emotional control, he convinces himself that all women are the problem. His partners become proxies for the anger he can never direct at his mother, ensuring that the cycle of blame, abuse, and control continues.

"Breaking free from this cycle would require deep introspection and the courage to dismantle the false narrative he has built around his mother. But for a narcissist, this level of self-awareness is nearly impossible. Admitting that his mother was at fault would mean admitting that he was powerless as a child, that he was used rather than loved, and that his suffering was never truly acknowledged. That level of vulnerability is something a narcissist cannot bear, so instead, he projects his rage onto the women in his life, punishing them for the sins of a mother he refuses to see as anything other than perfect."

Mother Wound and Misogyny

A male narcissist's misogyny is deeply rooted in his unresolved childhood wounds, particularly his relationship with his mother and the way he perceives women as a whole. His contempt for women is not just about arrogance or a superiority complex—it is a psychological defense mechanism, a projection of his own internalized resentment, fear, and inadequacy.

At the core of his misogyny is a deep-seated fear of female power. Whether he was controlled by an overbearing mother, neglected by an emotionally unavailable one, or witnessed his mother as a victim in his childhood home, his perception of women is shaped by the emotional turmoil he experienced in his formative years. If his mother was domineering, he learned early on that women use control, guilt, and emotional manipulation to get what they want. If she was weak or victimized, he saw women as helpless, needy, and emotionally draining. In both cases, he grows up resenting women—either because he believes they wield too much power or because he sees them as burdens.

This unresolved resentment manifests in his adult relationships, where he seeks to dominate a child. His need to assert dominance over women is not just about control—it is about revenge. He does not consciously acknowledge that his mother played a role in shaping his wounds; instead, he projects all his anger onto other women, making them pay for the powerlessness he once felt. This is why his relationships are built on manipulation, degradation, and emotional destruction.

Rather than addressing his trauma, he externalizes his pain, punishing his partner for the actions of the mother he refuses to hold accountable. To him, all women are either threats to his control or weak figures to be used and discarded. If his mother made him feel insignificant, he ensures that no woman ever makes him feel that way again by emotionally crippling them before they can ever challenge his superiority. If his mother played the role of a victim, he despises women who show vulnerability, viewing them as pathetic and unworthy of respect. Either way, his perception of women is twisted, and his interactions with them are driven by a toxic blend of contempt and entitlement.

His misogyny is not always overt. A covert narcissist may present himself as respectful, even charming, in public, but behind closed doors, his disdain for women seeps through in subtle but destructive ways. He undermines his partner's intelligence, dismisses her achievements, and minimizes her emotions, conditioning her to question her worth. He may enforce traditional gender roles, not out of genuine belief, but as a way to keep his partner in a submissive position where she is easier to control.

At his core, a male narcissist is threatened by a woman who is independent, confident, or self-sufficient, because she represents everything he fears—someone who cannot be manipulated, someone who will not accept his dominance without a fight. He will go to great lengths to break down a strong woman, using gaslighting, emotional withdrawal, and even financial control to strip her of her autonomy. His ultimate goal is not just to maintain power but to ensure that no woman ever has the ability to make him feel weak or insignificant again.

This misogyny is why many male narcissists have a pattern of devaluing and discarding women. Once a woman no longer serves his need for validation, or if she begins to see through his facade, he turns cruel, indifferent, and even vindictive. He seeks to humiliate her, tarnish her reputation and make her feel worthless, all to reinforce his belief that women are disposable and inferior. His hatred is fueled by his own inability to confront the real source of his suffering; his unresolved relationship with his mother. Until he acknowledges this, his cycle of abuse will continue, leaving a trail of broken partners who were never the true source of his rage, only the recipients of it.

CHAPTER 6

THE NARCISSISTIC FAMILY CULT

narcissistic family operates much like a cult, where the narcissistic parent or sometimes another dominant family member functions as the leader. In this dynamic, the family exists not as a nurturing unit but as a carefully controlled system designed to revolve around the narcissist's needs, desires, and ego. This type of environment can feel suffocating, confusing, and deeply invalidating for those caught in it.

In a narcissistic family, everything is about appearances. The family must project an image of perfection to the outside world, regardless of the dysfunction that exists behind closed doors. Any deviation from this façade is treated as betrayal. The narcissist uses guilt, manipulation, and fear to ensure loyalty and compliance, creating an environment where individuality is suppressed. You may find yourself unable to voice your opinions, make decisions freely, or even express emotions without fear of being punished, ridiculed, or ignored.

One of the hallmarks of a narcissistic family is the assignment of rigid roles. The narcissist will often designate a **golden child**, someone who is groomed to reflect their idealized self. This child becomes the trophy of the family, expected to excel and bring glory to the narcissist. On the other hand, there's the **scapegoat**—the family member who bears the blame for all the dysfunction and problems. The scapegoat often endures the brunt of the emotional abuse and is unfairly labeled as "the problem." Meanwhile, other family members may be relegated to being invisible, their needs overlooked entirely, or cast as enablers who maintain the status quo by siding with the narcissist.

Within this toxic system, boundaries don't exist. Privacy is disregarded, autonomy is denied, and any attempt to assert yourself is seen as a threat. Triangulation is a common tactic used by the narcissist to maintain control—pitting family members against each other to sow mistrust and keep the focus off their own abusive behavior. This creates a fractured environment where genuine connection between siblings or relatives is almost impossible. Instead, all relationships are filtered through the narcissist, ensuring their role as the center of power.

Living in this kind of environment leaves deep emotional scars. The constant invalidation, criticism, and manipulation erode your sense of self-worth. You might begin to question your perceptions, blame yourself for the family's dysfunction, or feel trapped in a cycle of guilt and obligation. Many of us, raised in narcissistic families, internalize these dynamics and struggle to recognize how deeply ingrained they are until much later in life.

Breaking free from a narcissistic family cult is no small task, but it is possible. It starts with recognizing the patterns, the rigid roles, the manipulation, the obsession with appearances and understanding that this is not your fault. The wounds left by this environment can feel overwhelming, but with time, support, and intentional effort, you can heal. Rebuilding your sense of identity, learning to set boundaries, and seeking validation outside of the family are all steps toward reclaiming your life.

The truth is, a narcissistic family act like a "**cult**" in its structure and control, but unlike a traditional cult, it can be even harder to leave because the ties are personal. However, understanding this dynamic is the first step to breaking free and creating a life that's truly yours—a life that honors your needs, your emotions, and your individuality.

> *Narcissistic parents always profess how much they love their children. When they have done nothing but ignore, abandon, degrade, insult and humiliate their child. The reality is, they resent the fact that society actually expects them to spend time with their kids and support them financially. The kids are used for show, that's it. These parents do not know what love is.*

Narcissistic family dynamics in narcissistic families, the child who upholds strong moral values is often singled out as the family's scapegoat. The truth-seeker becomes the adversary of those who are insincere. Being disliked for standing up for what is right and refusing to conform is a testament to your commitment to truth and integrity.

The Role of the Scapegoat in the Narcissistic Family Cult

In a narcissistic family, the scapegoat is the designated as "**problem**." This family member is unfairly blamed for all the dysfunction, failures, and emotional chaos within the family. The narcissist uses the scapegoat as a lightning rod to deflect attention from their own flaws and avoid taking accountability. The scapegoat becomes the emotional punching bag, absorbing the frustration, anger, and insecurities of the narcissist and sometimes even the other family members who join in to avoid becoming targets themselves.

If you've been the scapegoat, you know how isolating and painful this role can be. Nothing you do is ever enough. You're criticized for things beyond your control, and your achievements are either dismissed or minimized. The narcissist might say things like, "If it weren't for you, this family would be fine," or, "You're so selfish, just like your father/mother." Over time, this relentless blame can shatter your self-esteem and leave you feeling like you're inherently flawed.

Ironically, scapegoats are often the most emotionally aware members of the family. They're the ones who see through the narcissist's façade and recognize the dysfunction for what it is. This awareness makes them a threat to the narcissist, who seeks to maintain control by invalidating the scapegoat's perceptions and isolating them.

The scapegoat's role is particularly insidious because it's not just the narcissist targeting the other family members, desperate to avoid becoming the scapegoat themselves, may align with the narcissist and perpetuate the abuse. This creates a toxic dynamic where the scapegoat is ostracized, even by those who might privately agree with them.

The Cycle Breaker: Shattering Generational Patterns

While the scapegoat endures the brunt of the abuse, they often possess an inner strength and clarity that sets them apart. It's no coincidence that scapegoats are frequently the ones who eventually break free from the narcissistic family cult and challenge the cycle of abuse. These individuals are known as cycle breakers.

Being a cycle breaker is both a blessing and a burden. It's the act of stepping away from the toxic patterns ingrained in the family and choosing a different path—one of healing, self-awareness, and authenticity. Cycle breakers are the ones who refuse to perpetuate the lies, manipulation, and control that define the narcissistic family dynamic.

For the narcissist, a cycle breaker is a significant threat. They disrupt the status quo by rejecting the roles assigned to them and exposing the truth about the family's dysfunction. This often leads to retaliation, smear campaigns, attempts to discredit their experiences, and efforts to pull them back into the fold through guilt or manipulation. The narcissist will say things like, "You've changed," or, "After everything I've done for you, how could you abandon us?"

But breaking the cycle is an act of courage. It requires immense self-awareness and resilience to confront the painful realities of your upbringing and choose to heal. As a cycle breaker, you might feel like you're walking this path alone, but in doing so, you're not only liberating yourself—you're creating a legacy of change. You're rewriting the narrative for future generations, ensuring that the patterns of abuse, blame, and control don't continue.

How Narcissistic Parents Weaponize Children Against The Scapegoat Or Cycle Breaker

Narcissistic parents often employ deeply damaging tactics to manipulate their children against the scapegoat or cycle breaker in the family. For a narcissist, control is everything, and they will not hesitate to weaponize their children to maintain their dominance and punish anyone who challenges their authority or disrupts the family dynamic. This manipulation can be subtle yet pervasive, creating divisions that isolate the scapegoat further while reinforcing the narcissist's power.

When a scapegoat or cycle breaker begins to assert boundaries, express their independence, or call out the dysfunction in the family, the narcissistic parent perceives this as an act of betrayal. To retaliate, they start by gaslighting the children, twisting the narrative to portray the scapegoat as the villain. They may rewrite events, exaggerate conflicts, or fabricate lies, painting the scapegoat as selfish, unstable, or unloving. The narcissist often assumes the role of the victim, convincing the children that they have been wronged and that the scapegoat is the source of the family's troubles. Phrases like, "They've abandoned us" or "They only think about themselves" are commonly used to distort reality and garner the children's loyalty.

Triangulation becomes another powerful tool in their arsenal. Narcissistic parents strategically sow discord by sharing selective information, pitting siblings against one another or turning them against the scapegoat. This ensures that alliances within the family are fractured, leaving the scapegoat isolated and unsupported. Children who side with the narcissist are rewarded with praise, affection, or material gifts, reinforcing their dependence on the parent. Conversely, the scapegoat is punished through criticism, blame, or exclusion, creating a dynamic in which the children learn that siding with the scapegoat could result in their own marginalization.

Over time, the children become emotionally dependent on the narcissistic parent. By undermining their confidence and decision-making abilities, the narcissist ensures that the children look to them for validation and guidance. This emotional manipulation fosters loyalty, making it difficult for the children to see the scapegoat's perspective or recognize the narcissist's toxic behavior. The scapegoat's attempts to encourage independence or critical thinking are often framed as selfishness or as attempts to break up the family.

For the scapegoat or cycle breaker, this manipulation is profoundly isolating. Being turned into the family's villain by both the narcissistic parent and the children can deepen feelings of loneliness and reinforce the belief that they are inherently flawed or unlovable. However, the impact on the children is equally damaging. They grow up trapped in a web of manipulation, unable to form their own opinions or relationships, and burdened by a loyalty to a parent who uses them as pawns rather than truly nurturing their well-being.

Healing as a Scapegoat and Cycle Breaker

The journey from scapegoat to cycle breaker is transformative but challenging. It often involves:

- **Recognizing the Pattern:** Understanding that you were unfairly targeted and that the family dysfunction is not your fault.

- **Setting Boundaries:** Learning to protect your emotional and physical well-being by establishing firm boundaries with the narcissist and enablers.

- **Seeking Validation Elsewhere:** Building relationships outside the family that are rooted in mutual respect and genuine care.

- **Processing the Pain:** Working through the grief, anger, and sadness of being scapegoated. This can involve therapy, journaling, or other healing practices.

- **Embracing Self-Worth:** Reclaiming your sense of value and learning to celebrate your strengths, talents, and individuality.

- **Finding Your Voice:** Speaking your truth and sharing your story, not to convince the narcissist or their enablers, but to validate your own experiences and inspire others on similar journeys.

The Impact on the Scapegoat and the Children

For the scapegoat or cycle breaker, this tactic is profoundly isolating and painful. They may feel betrayed by their siblings or even their own children, who have been manipulated into seeing them as the enemy. This can deepen feelings of loneliness and reinforce the scapegoat's belief that they are somehow inherently flawed.

For the children, the impact is equally damaging. They are robbed of the opportunity to form their own opinions and relationships, forced instead to adopt the narcissist's perspective. They may grow up feeling confused, manipulated, or burdened by loyalty to a parent who doesn't truly have their best interests at heart.

Support vs Control in Narcissist Family Cult

Respect vs Domination

- Support: Respects your choices and decisions.
- Control: Forces their opinions and decisions on you.

Encouragement vs Manipulation

- Support: Motivates you to achieve your goals.
- Control: Manipulates you into fulfilling their desires.

Autonomy vs Dependency

- Support: Encourages independence and self-reliance.
- Control: Creates dependency and restricts freedom.

Open Communication vs Guilt-Tripping

- Support: Welcomes honest discussions.
- Control: Uses guilt to suppress your voice.

Unconditional Love vs Conditional Approval

- Support: Accepts you for who you are.
- Control: Offers approval based on compliance.

Narcissist as Parents

Narcissistic parents view their children not as individuals with their own rights, needs, and emotions, but as extensions of themselves—tools to manipulate and control, both as a means to bolster their own image and to exert power over their spouse. For them, children serve as pawns in an ongoing game, carefully placed to secure their sense of superiority and maintain dominance. They don't see their children's feelings, aspirations, or identities—instead, they see opportunities to control, manipulate, and fuel their own desires for attention and admiration.

From the outside, a narcissistic parent may appear affectionate or loving, but beneath the surface lies a deep, toxic need to shape their children into their personal "narcissistic supply"—a source of admiration and validation. These children are expected to be perfect, constantly serving the narcissist's emotional needs, while their own needs are ignored or minimized. The narcissist demands complete loyalty and compliance from their children, viewing them not as independent beings, but as accessories or tools to maintain control.

Emotional abuse is central to the narcissist's manipulation. They will use guilt, shame, and fear to keep their children tethered to them, fostering dependency while eroding their self-esteem. Narcissists often engage in a practice known as triangulation, where they pit children against each other or against their spouse, creating competition for their affection and validation. This leaves children feeling confused, unsupported, and often unsure of where they stand. They learn to distrust their own feelings as their emotions are constantly dismissed or twisted to serve the narcissist's agenda.

A common tactic is gaslighting, where a narcissistic parent will undermine a child's perception of reality. If a child expresses hurt or confusion about something the parent has done, the narcissist deny their actions or accuse the child of being overly sensitive, irrational, or selfish or telling lies. This manipulation makes the child question their own thoughts and feelings, leaving them in a state of perpetual emotional instability. As the child grows, they may develop deep feelings of inadequacy, believing they are never good enough for the narcissist, and constantly striving for approval that will never come.

Narcissistic parents also utilize emotional neglect, where the child's emotional needs are completely ignored or dismissed. These parents fail to provide the necessary affection, guidance, and validation that children need to grow into emotionally healthy adults. Instead, the narcissist's needs always come first, and the child is often forced to adopt an adult-like role of caregiver or emotional support, sacrificing their own well-being for the narcissist's comfort.

The emotional toll of growing up with a narcissistic parent is often profound. Children of narcissists are more likely to struggle with anxiety, depression, low self-esteem, and self-doubt as they try to navigate the confusing and painful dynamics in their home. They often feel as though they are never enough, constantly trying to earn love or approval that is elusive or conditional. Narcissistic abuse in childhood can leave scars that last a lifetime, impacting how they form relationships, trust others, and even view themselves.

By the time they reach adulthood, these children may struggle with emotional regulation and boundary setting because they were never taught how to recognize their own emotions, let alone express them in healthy ways. They may have difficulty identifying toxic patterns in relationships, unknowingly gravitating toward narcissistic partners, repeating the cycle of abuse.

Ultimately, the narcissistic parent's primary goal is to maintain control—and their child is just another tool in that effort. Emotional abuse is used to break down their child's sense of self, to make them feel worthless, so that they can be more easily controlled. The narcissist does not see their children as human beings with their own hopes, dreams, or emotions. To them, their children are simply a means to an end, existing solely to reinforce their own power and control.

Narcissistic parents can be deeply envious of their own children, particularly when they see qualities, achievements, or traits in their children that they themselves lack or fear. This envy often stems from the narcissist's own insecurities, sense of inadequacy, and constant need to be the canter of attention. Because of this, they may consciously or subconsciously try to sabotage their child's self-esteem, development, and overall happiness, ultimately impacting their child's life in damaging ways.

The long-term consequences of growing up in this environment are devastating. The narcissist creates a world where their child is left emotionally shattered, confused, and feeling alone, with the constant pressure to please and seek approval from someone who is incapable of offering love or understanding in return.

CHAPTER 7

DIVORCING NARCISSIST-DEHUMANIZATION AND THE DISCARD PHASE

Divorcing a narcissist is one of the most emotionally and mentally grueling experiences a person can face. For a narcissist, the end of a relationship isn't a mutual parting but a battle for domination, where they aim to control, punish, and dehumanize their partner. The discard phase is a calculated effort to strip their victim of identity, independence, and dignity, leaving them feeling powerless and broken. The discard phase is the worst and the most painful part of narcissistic abuse because this is where the narcissist reveals their true intent to destroy you.

When the Narcissist Knows You've Figured Them Out

Once the narcissist realizes you've seen through their facade, they will stop at nothing to destroy you. Their need to safeguard their public image becomes their primary objective, and they will go to any lengths to protect their carefully curated persona. They are masters of manipulation and will use your own children as tools to pull your strings.

It's not uncommon for them to weaponize your role as a parent: *"If you tell anyone, I'll ruin this child's future or take them away from you."* They thrive on the fear and anguish this creates, ensuring you stay silent while they continue their campaign of destruction. At the same time portraying a loving and caring father image for the outside world.

Legal Abuse and False Documentation

The narcissist doesn't stop at threats—they escalate to using legal systems and false documentation to ruin you. From filing baseless accusations to manipulating legal procedures, they aim to trap you in an endless cycle of litigation. This is not just about control, it's about stripping you of your life, resources and sense of security.

They create false narratives, submit fraudulent documents, and use the legal system as a weapon to exhaust you emotionally, financially, and mentally. This deliberate abuse ensures you're too consumed by survival to rebuild or fight back effectively. They use baiting to provoke the victim and put false allegations on them to make their case stronger and portray themselves as victims.

Narcissists use messages and emails to create a false record, documenting events that never happened or expressing fake affection for their children. This tactic is intended to build a fabricated narrative they can use to manipulate situations, especially in legal or custody matters, or to present a caring image to others. Keeping clear records of actual events, using neutral language, and involving a mediator when possible can help counter these false claims.

They suddenly become more affectionate towards the children, carefully documenting every interaction with them to build a legal advantage.

Narcissists pursue full custody of their children not out of genuine love or desire to bond with them, but as a way to maintain control. For many narcissists, custody battles are less about the well-being of the children and more about safeguarding their image, protecting their own interests, and denying the other parent any sense of victory. This desire for custody stems from their need to control, win at all costs, and project a certain image to the outside world.

Narcissists view divorce and custody proceedings as competitions. They feel that **"winning"** full custody will humiliate or punish their ex-partner, proving they are in control. This desire to "win" can be so powerful that it overrides any genuine concern for their child's needs or well-being.

Once they have custody, narcissistic parents use the children as leverage against their ex-partner, controlling and manipulating interactions to maintain their power. They will withhold visits, enforce unreasonable restrictions, or dictate terms that suit their agenda. This allows them to keep their ex-partner in an emotional bind, prolonging the abuse cycle.

The narcissist will use law to abuse you further, **they will get you arrested with false accusations just as a coercive tactic.** This is a strategy to divert attention from their abuse and to support their narrative that it has been you not them.

Narcissists are really crafty and manipulative, they can twist the truth in their favor like no other. They are especially good at finding **loopholes** in court documents and orders. They will attack your character, your life choices, and your parenting. They also work very hard at presenting a "saintly" imagine, so many people will be fooled including law professionals who do not have experience working with narcissist or any cluster b personalities.

Financial Abuse: The Silent Chain That Keeps You Trapped

Financial manipulation remains one of their most insidious tools. They continue their campaign of control by starving the victim of resources and depriving of basic necessities like food, clothing and shelter. By withholding money or refusing to pay for essentials, they push the victim to a state of deprivation. They manipulate false narratives to portray themselves as the sole provider for the family's financial needs, making it extremely difficult for the victim to prove their side of the story.

Then, they begin limiting your ability to earn. They may discourage you from working, saying, "You don't need to work—I'll take care of everything." At first, it sounds like love and generosity, but the underlying motive is control.

The moment you stop earning your own income, they have you exactly where they want you, dependent.

Over time, they make you feel incompetent with money. They micromanage your spending, scrutinize every purchase, and question your financial decisions. Suddenly, asking for money feels like begging, and when you do, you're met with accusations of being irresponsible, selfish, or ungrateful. They start controlling what you eat, what you wear, and whether you can afford basic necessities.

As the cycle worsens, they become stingy—not with themselves, but with you. You may find yourself deprived of essentials, unable to buy a single piece of clothing, while they continue to spend freely on their own wants. They withhold money as a form of punishment, making sure you feel the weight of their control. And when the discard phase arrives, the cruelty escalates, they stop providing altogether, leaving you and your children to fend for yourselves, knowing you have nowhere to turn.

This is enslavement. A narcissist's goal is to make you financially helpless so that leaving feels impossible

This abuse often starts long before the divorce, with tactics like discouraging you from working or sabotaging your career. But in the discard phase, it intensifies. They may rack up debts in your name, refuse to pay **child support**, or delay legal proceedings to drain your finances. The goal is clear, to leave you powerless, struggling for survival, and dependent on them. Signs of financial abuse could look like:

- Interfering with your performance at work or sabotaging employment opportunities by calling the victim at work while you are busy, visiting the workplace unannounced or causing them to lose their job.
- Becoming enraged over money expenditures followed by verbal and emotional abuse.
- Controlling how the money is spent.
- Making the reimbursement for the children's expenses extremely difficult.

- Narcs train you to not ask for financial favours.

- Hiding assets, investments, funds and personal expenditures.

- Ruining your credit history,

- strategically draining your finances.

- Withholding funds for the victim or children to obtain basic needs such as food and medicines.

- Evading or refusing to pay for child support and dragging out divorce proceedings to cripple you financially.

Through financial abuse, they become so cold and calculated that they will push you to the brink—depriving you of everything, from basic necessities to any form of emotional support, to **"teach you a lesson."** Their cruelty knows no bounds, and they will ensure you are stripped of any means to escape or rebuild.

Survivor Story:

Sarah had once believed that leaving was the hardest part. That if she could just step away from the suffocating grip of Daniel's control, she would find relief. But freedom, she soon realized, was not as simple as walking out the door. It was a battle she had to fight on every front—financially, emotionally, and legally.

Daniel had made the rules clear. As long as she endured his abuse, she could stay. She and their child could eat, sleep under a roof, and exist—under his terms. But the moment she took a stand, the moment she refused to submit, he took it all away. No money for food, no money for their child's needs, no money for rent. Every bill became a weapon, every empty fridge shelf a reminder that he dictated her survival. It wasn't just Daniel—this was how the world worked, especially in narcissistic abuse. **Submission meant survival. Resistance meant exile.**

In a foreign country with no family to fall back on, Sarah had no choice but to find work—any work to keep herself and her child afloat. Sarah had to take a job far below her potential. The corridors were filled with whispered insults, the weight of being an outsider pressing down on her every day. The racism was unspoken yet deafening, and the sexual harassment was constant leering stares, inappropriate jokes, lingering touches. She gritted her teeth and bore it all because there was no other option. She had to survive. Her child had to survive.

But as she fought her way through each day, the legal system failed her in the same breath. She pleaded for justice, for recognition of the abuse, but she was met with indifference. Papers were shuffled, cases were delayed, and her suffering was reduced to mere technicalities. She was gaslit at every turn—told that she was exaggerating, that she should be grateful she had a roof over her head, that perhaps she was the problem. Society too played its part, questioning her choices, doubting her truth and expecting her to endure silently, just as so many women before her had been forced to.

But Sarah was not like them. She would not be erased. She didn't want her daughter to be the victim of Daniel's abuse.

Every paycheck she earned, every meal she put on the table, every morning she woke up determined to fight another day was an act of defiance. Daniel had tried to strip her of dignity, of agency, of hope—but she held onto them with everything she had. And though the wounds of financial abuse, discrimination, and legal betrayal cut deep, they shattered her and her daughter in ways the world could not see. The weight of survival left scars on both of them, shaping their days with uncertainty and fear.

Isolation and Public Humiliation

Narcissists are skilled at isolating their victims. During the discard phase, they amplify this tactic by spreading lies and manipulating those around you. Friends, family, and even colleagues will be turned against you through carefully crafted stories that position the narcissist as the victim and you as unstable or abusive.

This triangulation not only isolates you but also gaslights you into doubting your own reality. Meanwhile—in public, they maintain their charming persona, ensuring no one suspects the truth behind their actions.

Emotional and Psychological Dehumanization

In the discard phase, every vulnerability you have is weaponized against you. Narcissists deliberately mock your pain, dismiss your feelings, and attack the things that bring you joy, your hobbies, passions, or even your relationship with your children.

If children are involved, they become pawns in the narcissist's game. They may withhold access, alienate the child, or create custody battles designed to emotionally and financially exhaust you. This ensures maximum control while inflicting the greatest possible harm.

What makes this phase particularly devastating is the narcissist's intent. Their actions are calculated, not emotional. For them, the divorce isn't an end—it's another arena to assert dominance and prove their superiority. They thrive on watching you struggle, knowing they have the upper hand.

Through every tactic, from emotional manipulation to financial control, the narcissist ensures that they remain the one in charge—even if they have to destroy you in the process. Their cruelty is relentless, and their refusal to let go of power is all-consuming.

Secretive Life of a Narcissist

Narcissists are masters at leading double lives, especially when it comes to their romantic relationships. Behind the charm, the grand promises, and the carefully crafted public image, there is often a secretive love life that fuels their insatiable need for control, validation, and excitement.

Imagine a person who thrives on attention like oxygen. For a narcissist, one source of admiration is never enough, they crave variety, drama, and the thrill of keeping people guessing. This is why many narcissists juggle multiple relationships, often without their primary partner having the slightest clue. They are adept at compartmentalizing, keeping each part of their lives separate, like pieces of a puzzle only they know how to assemble.

A narcissist's secretive love life often stems from their deep insecurity and inability to form authentic connections. They may present themselves as devoted partners in public while simultaneously engaging in affairs, emotionally manipulating others, or pursuing attention online. Social media and dating apps become their playgrounds, anonymous spaces where they can charm, flirt, and exploit, feeding their ego without the constraints of accountability.

If caught, they will deny everything, sometimes even in the face of overwhelming evidence. Gaslighting becomes their weapon of choice. They'll accuse their partner of being paranoid or controlling, turning the focus away from their actions and onto their partner's supposed flaws. It's a calculated move to maintain the upper hand while sowing seeds of self-doubt in the other person.

Secrecy is essential to the narcissist. It gives them the power to maintain a facade of perfection while indulging their darker impulses behind the scenes. They relish the idea of being the puppet master, pulling the strings and knowing that no one can fully uncover their hidden life. This secrecy isn't just about avoiding consequences—it's about control. As long as they can keep you guessing, they remain in charge of the narrative.

What's more, the narcissist's secret love life isn't always about physical infidelity. Emotional affairs are equally common. They'll seek out admirers who validate their image, provide an emotional high, or reinforce their belief that they are desirable and powerful. These emotional entanglements can feel just as violating as a physical affair because they are a betrayal of trust and intimacy.

For those in relationships with narcissists, discovering this hidden side can be devastating. The realization that the person you trusted is capable of such deception shakes your sense of reality. Narcissists, however, will twist this moment into an opportunity to victimize themselves. They might claim they were driven to cheat or that they felt neglected, redirecting the blame onto you or external circumstances.

It's important to understand that their secretive love life isn't about you—it's about them. Their need for constant stimulation, admiration, and control drives these behaviors. They lack the ability to form genuine emotional bonds, so they seek fulfillment through multiple shallow connections, leaving chaos in their wake.

Recognizing these patterns can be liberating. Once you understand that their secrecy and deceit are part of their deeply rooted need for power and validation, you can begin to detach from their manipulation. Protect yourself by setting boundaries, seeking support, and refusing to play into their games. You don't have to live under the shadow of their double life.

An Envious Narcissist

An envious narcissist is consumed by a deep sense of inadequacy masked by arrogance and entitlement. They cannot tolerate the success, happiness, or even the simplest joys of others as these feel like direct threats to their fragile ego. Instead of celebrating someone else's achievements, they diminish, criticize, or sabotage them to restore their perceived superiority. Beneath their smug facade lies a festering resentment—they crave what others have, yet they cannot admit their envy. This makes them particularly dangerous, as they're often relentless in their attempts to tear others down to elevate themselves.

Narcissist has contempt for people they are jealous of and it does not matter if you are their spouse, friend or even their own children. Narcissists feel entitled and more deserving than other people and it does not matter who it is. As insane as it sounds if there is something that they envy about, they will want to **destroy** you. They suffer from **pathological envy**. Another reason they are so rough with victims and push them around is because it makes them feel powerful and in control. That's how they get their ego boost and narcissistic supply.

Downplaying or Sabotaging Success: They dismiss your achievements or belittle them, making passive-aggressive comments to undermine your confidence.

Copying Your Accomplishments: Envious narcissists mimic what you do to feel better about themselves. They steal your ideas, achievements, or lifestyle in an attempt to overshadow your success.

Undermining Your Efforts: They create obstacles or spread negative rumors about you to discredit your work or achievements. This can also involve covert actions that sabotage your plans or goals.

Exaggerated Displays of Superiority: In response to their jealousy, they try to outshine you in exaggerated ways by bragging or flaunting their own (real or imagined) successes.

Lack of Genuine Support: They will rarely celebrate your victories or offer genuine encouragement. Instead, they pretend to care while secretly feeling resentful or trying to one-up you.

Projecting Insecurity: They accuse you of being envious or insecure, projecting their own feelings onto you in an attempt to deflect from their own jealousy.

Ruining Special events: Narcissists have a way of ruining special events, especially occasions like your birthday, where the attention naturally shifts away from them. They create unnecessary drama, pick a fight, or act dismissive to ensure the day doesn't go smoothly. This behavior stems from their inability to handle someone else being in the spotlight. By sabotaging your happiness, they regain a sense of control and ensure the focus eventually shifts back to them, leaving you feeling hurt and disappointed on what should have been your special day.

Narcissist Introjection

Narcissists subconsciously copy abusive behavior they've witnessed or experienced, internalizing it as a survival or control mechanism. They may project these behaviors onto others, assuming people will act similarly. For instance, if they've seen someone being deceitful or manipulative, they might believe others will do the same to them, leading to distrust and preemptive defensive tactics like gaslighting or manipulation. This behavior reflects their deep-seated fears and inability to process past trauma healthily. Trauma repetition or repetition compulsion explains how narcissists subconsciously repeat abusive patterns they've been exposed to in their own past.

Targeting your values and Principles

Narcissists are highly skilled at identifying and targeting your core values and principles, because these are the very things that make you feel grounded and secure in your beliefs. They do this with precision, as they understand that by manipulating or exploiting your values, they can control your emotions and behaviors to maintain their own dominance in the relationship.

From the very beginning, they pay close attention to what matters most to you—whether it's your family, your integrity, your kindness or your sense of justice. Once they've identified these core values, they start to use them against you. They may feign interest or agreement with your beliefs to gain your trust and affection, mirroring your values to create the illusion of compatibility.

However, once they have you hooked, they begin to subtly undermine or manipulate your values. They might challenge your principles, try to twist them to serve their own agenda, or make you feel guilty for holding firm to what you believe. For example, if you're a person who values honesty, a narcissist may use deceit as a tool to control you, constantly testing the limits of your tolerance for dishonesty. They might gaslight you into questioning your own perception of truth, eroding your sense of reality and leaving you in a constant state of doubt.

> *If you're someone who deeply values loyalty, the narcissist may push you to the brink of betrayal, manipulating situations where you're forced to compromise your integrity, making you feel conflicted or even guilty for upholding your values. They target your sense of self-worth, slowly warping your beliefs to make you question your judgment, your trust in others, and your ability to make sound decisions.*

The more they undermine your core values, the more they weaken your ability to stand firm in your beliefs. This is how they establish control. Narcissists thrive on creating dependency, and by attacking your values, they weaken your sense of autonomy, making you more susceptible to their manipulation. They feed off the power they gain by distorting your moral compass, leaving you constantly trying to balance your integrity with their demands.

In essence, narcissists target your values and principles not because they believe in them, but because they know that once they can manipulate them, they've gained the ability to control you emotionally and psychologically.

Baiting

Baiting is a form of manipulation that narcissists use to provoke an emotional response from their target. In the context of narcissistic abuse, baiting often involves subtle verbal tactics designed to trigger an emotional reaction or defensive response. **The narcissist will say something calculated to provoke you, then record your reaction (either directly or indirectly) to use it as evidence later, especially in legal matters.**

Narcissists who engage in baiting often have a hidden agenda, they seek to provoke reactions that can later be used as evidence in legal matters, such as custody battles, divorce proceedings, or legal disputes. They often create situations where your emotional reaction can be used against you. Here's how this process unfolds:

Provoking an Emotional Reaction:

The narcissist will use the verbal bait to provoke an emotional response from you, knowing that your reaction could make you appear unhinged, unstable, or overly emotional.

Twisting the Narrative:

After baiting you into reacting, the narcissist may then manipulate the situation, presenting the reaction as evidence of your emotional instability, aggression, or inability to co-parent. For instance, they might record your reaction (either by taking notes, recording a conversation secretly, or using witnesses) and claim that you're volatile or difficult to deal with.

Weaponizing the Emotional Response:

If there's an ongoing legal issue, such as child custody or divorce proceedings, the narcissist may bring up your emotional reaction as **"proof"** that you're incapable of handling the situation or co-parenting effectively. They may say things like:

> *"They yelled at me for no reason during the meeting."*
> *"I've had to endure emotional abuse from them. They constantly fly off the handle."*

This makes it difficult for the victim, because the narcissist has controlled the narrative to make them appear in a negative light.

Exaggerating or Fabricating Details:

Narcissists are also known to exaggerate or fabricate details about your emotional response. They may claim that you were aggressive, out of control, or unreasonable, painting you as the antagonist in the situation. They could use these exaggerated claims in court documents, testimonies, or communication with lawyers.

Creating the "Evidence":

Narcissists may subtly encourage others to witness and validate their fabricated version of events, making it more difficult for you to disprove the claims in legal settings. This could include family members, friends, or even mutual acquaintances who've been manipulated to align with the narcissist's narrative.

How to Protect Yourself from Baiting and Recording Manipulation

- **Stay Calm and Detached:** Recognize when baiting is occurring and try not to react emotionally. Remain calm and composed, even if they provoke you.

- **Document Your Own Side:** Keep a detailed journal of conversations, incidents, and your emotional reactions. Record your own version of events so that you have evidence to counter the narcissist's version.

- **Avoid Arguing in Private:** Be mindful of the fact that a narcissist might try to record your emotional response. Whenever possible, avoid arguing in private, especially in emotionally charged situations. If they insist on having a conversation, try to make sure it's in a public space or a setting with neutral parties present.

- **Seek Legal Advice:** If you suspect that the narcissist is using baiting to manipulate legal matters, seek legal advice about how to handle the situation. A lawyer can help you understand how to protect yourself and your interests during custody or divorce proceedings.

- **Set Boundaries:** Be clear about boundaries with the narcissist and stick to them. If they attempt to bait you into an emotional reaction, disengage calmly and assertively.

By understanding the baiting tactics used by covert narcissists and knowing how to respond, you can protect yourself and avoid falling into their manipulative traps. Recognizing this behavior in advance will help you stay focused and keep your emotions in check, especially in situations that could be used against you legally.

Smear Campaign

A smear campaign during a divorce with a narcissist is a calculated and malicious effort to destroy your reputation, isolate you from support, and manipulate legal systems to paint you as the abuser while they present themselves as the victim. This is not just an emotional attack, it is a well-planned psychological and social assault designed to discredit you and shift the narrative in their favor.

The narcissist's ultimate goal is control. They don't just want to "win" the divorce- they want to ensure that you lose in every possible way emotionally, socially, financially, and even legally. To do this, they use deception, manipulation, and a carefully crafted strategy to turn friends, family, and even professionals such as lawyers, therapists, and court officials against you.

One of their primary tactics is spreading **partial truths, exaggerated stories, and outright lies**. They may take a small, insignificant fact from your past and distort it just enough to make it sound damning. By adding exaggerated or fabricated details, they craft a narrative that makes you seem unstable, aggressive, or even abusive. They cherry-pick moments from your history, completely stripping them of context, and present a version of events that supports their false claims. The genius of this strategy lies in the mix of truth and lies—it makes it much harder for you to defend yourself because you're constantly stuck justifying or explaining your past actions instead of exposing their deception.

They may frame the story as though they are "concerned" about you, saying things like–*"I just don't know what's happened to them lately... they seem so angry and unpredictable."* This creates doubt in people's minds, and before you know it, those who once supported you start distancing themselves, unsure of whom to believe.

The next step in the smear campaign is manipulating the legal system. Narcissists are masters at playing the victim, and they know exactly how to present themselves as the "reasonable" or "innocent" party. They may file false police reports, make misleading statements to social workers or child custody evaluators, or even create fake documentation to support their claims. If they can provoke you into an emotional reaction; especially in a recorded conversation or text message they will use it as "evidence" to claim that you are unstable, irrational, or even dangerous.

This is particularly dangerous in custody battles, where a narcissist can weaponize your emotions and reactions to portray you as an unfit parent. They might claim that you are emotionally volatile, neglectful, or even abusive, despite the fact that they are the ones engaging in manipulation and coercion behind the scenes.

The smear campaign also extends to professionals involved in the legal process. The narcissist will carefully craft their persona when dealing with lawyers, judges, mediators, and therapists, presenting themselves as the rational, composed, and suffering party, while painting you as the unpredictable and problematic one. They will use charm, tears, and even fake humility to gain sympathy while ensuring that you are seen in the worst possible light.

If you find yourself in the middle of this kind of attack, it is essential to remain calm and strategic. Do not engage emotionally with the narcissist, no matter how much they provoke you. Instead, document everything, every email, every message, every interaction. Keep records of your own communication and interactions with mutual contacts to counter false claims. If possible, seek legal and professional advice to protect yourself from their tactics.

The narcissistic partner will oppose you for whatever you want to do even if its in their favour. Their whole objective is to get a supply and reaction from you and make your life miserable which fuels them.

> *"Most importantly, trust in the truth. The narcissist thrives on deception, but their lies can only hold for so long. Over time, their inconsistencies will catch up with them, and those who were fooled by*

their smear campaign will begin to see the cracks in their story. Until then, focus on safeguarding your mental and emotional well-being, and don't waste your energy trying to convince those who have already been manipulated. The best revenge against a narcissist's smear campaign is living well and refusing to play into their game."

Spying and Snooping

A spying narcissist invades your privacy in discreet ways, often using covert surveillance to gather information about you. This can include:

- **Monitoring your digital activity** – Checking your emails, messages, call logs, or social media without your knowledge. They might do this by secretly accessing your devices, guessing passwords, or even installing spyware.

- **Physically snooping** – Searching through your personal belongings, diaries, or documents when you're not around.

- **Gathering information from third parties** – Manipulating mutual friends, colleagues, or even your own child into revealing details about your life.

- **Eavesdropping** – Listening in on your conversations or using hidden recording devices.

- Covert narcissists spy for control, manipulation, and blackmail. Their goal is to collect information that they can later use against you in subtle yet damaging ways.

- **Control** – They want to know what you're doing, thinking, or planning so they can stay one step ahead and maintain power over you.

- **Manipulation** – They use the information to gaslight you, twist your words, or create smear campaigns.

- **Blackmail** – If they find something they believe could damage your reputation, they hold it over you as leverage to keep you compliant.

This behavior is a serious violation of personal boundaries. Covert narcissists lack respect for your privacy because they see you as an extension of themselves, not as an independent individual. Their need for control overrides any sense of ethical or moral responsibility.

> *"Unlike overt narcissists, who might openly demand information, a covert narcissist works in the shadows. Their methods are secretive, deceptive and indirect, which makes them more dangerous in some ways. They won't confront you directly but will collect data in the background, carefully curating a false sense of trust while they spy."*

Counter Parenting

Undermine the other parent's authority: They actively encourage the child to defy the other parent's rules, disregarding boundaries and discipline in favor of giving the child what they want—just to "stick it" to the other parent. They openly disrespect the other parent in front of the child, fostering misbehavior toward the other parent and asserting dominance within the household. This deliberate act of demeaning the other parent is a calculated effort to undermine their authority and influence.

Create competition with the other parent: The narcissist will make sure the child sees them as the "fun" parent who allows them to break the rules, framing the other parent as strict or controlling. This pits the child against the other parent, making them resentful and less likely to respect their authority.

Sabotage the other parent's relationship with the child: They may manipulate the child into rejecting time with the other parent, claiming the child is "too tired" or "doesn't want to go." They may deliberately create scheduling conflicts or emotionally manipulate the child to stay with them, making the child feel like it's a choice.

They actively create a rift between the child and the other parent by undermining the latter's authority and trust. For instance, if the other parent assigns a task to the child, they covertly dismiss it, telling the child it's unimportant and doesn't need to be done. They may go as far as portraying the other parent as harmful or untrustworthy, warning the child to be cautious around them—ironically concealing the fact that they themselves pose the greatest danger to the child's emotional well-being.

These behaviors can cause significant emotional harm to the child, as they are torn between two conflicting influences—the narcissistic parent's manipulative tactics and the healthy parenting of the other parent. Over time, this confusion can lead to the child developing dysfunctional attachment patterns, emotional instability, and difficulty trusting their own instincts.

> *"Narcissist will deliberately neglect their parental duties and then make false claims that you are the one alienating the children from them"*

These strategies are designed to manipulate the child into believing that the narcissistic parent is the "better" parent who genuinely cares for their well-being, while painting the other parent as evil, uncaring, or even hateful toward the child. By doing so, they seek to gain the child's confidence and loyalty. The child is then used as a tool to manipulate and emotionally control the other parent indirectly when direct control is no longer possible. This behavior often surfaces during the divorce or discard phase, as the narcissistic parent aims to safeguard their image in court or within the legal system. It's a calculated move to weaponize the child against the other parent while maintaining an illusion of being the "ideal" caregiver.

The narcissist's ultimate goal in using these tactics is to create a divide-and-conquer strategy within the family, isolating the other parent from the child and weakening the child's emotional bond with the parent who poses the greatest threat to their control. To a narcissistic parent, children are often viewed as mere pawns rather than individuals with their own needs and emotions. They are tools to be used for personal gain, whether to assert control over the other parent, maintain a façade of superiority, or protect their own interests in legal or social situations.

Parental Alienation

In the case of a *"divorcing narcissist"*, children can become pawns in the battle for control. The narcissist use the child to manipulate the other parent, creating rifts between the family unit. This is often accompanied by parental alienation, where the narcissist tries to turn the child against the other parent by spreading lies and fostering resentment. This emotional manipulation is a tactic to weaken the other parent's bond with the child and maintain control over the child's loyalty.

Parental Alienation is one of the most destructive and insidious tactics employed by narcissistic parents to maintain control over their children and sabotage the other parent's relationship with them. It involves intentionally creating a rift between the child and the other parent, often through lies, manipulation, and subtle emotional abuse. For narcissists, parental alienation serves as a means of power and control, furthering their ability to dominate and manipulate their family dynamics.

A narcissistic parent uses parental alienation to assert dominance over the child and undermine the authority of the other parent, typically the one they see as a threat or rival. They may do this by portraying the targeted parent as unfit, untrustworthy, or even abusive—despite no evidence to support their claims. The goal is to manipulate the child into believing that the other parent is the enemy, making them feel guilt or confusion about their love and loyalty. This process often involves subtle tactics, including:

Lying about the other parent: The narcissist will make up stories or exaggerate the other parent's flaws, portraying them as neglectful, emotionally unstable, or uncaring.

Undermining the other parent's authority: The narcissist may openly disrespect or criticize the targeted parent in front of the child, sending the message that they do not deserve the child's respect or affection.

Creating false loyalty tests: They will often demand the child's loyalty and make them feel guilty for spending time with the other parent, framing it as a betrayal. If the child expresses love or affection for the other parent, the narcissist may react with anger or disdain, reinforcing the idea that the child must choose sides.

Gaslighting the child: Narcissists will manipulate the child's perception of events, denying the child's reality or rewriting history to make the targeted parent seem like the villain.

Emotionally blackmailing the child: They may create scenarios where the child feels responsible for the narcissist's emotional well-being, using guilt to manipulate them into rejecting the other parent.

As a result, the child begins to internalize these messages, often developing deep emotional confusion and conflicted feelings about both parents. The narcissist is able to turn the child into an ally, pitting them against the targeted parent and diminishing the child's ability to have a healthy, balanced relationship with both caregivers.

Counter Parenting refers to the narcissist's use of the child to specifically counteract or undermine the efforts of the other parent. While parental alienation focuses on creating emotional distance between the child and the targeted parent, counter parenting is more about actively working against the other parent's authority, often in direct opposition to their decisions, values, and parenting style. Narcissists use this tactic to ensure they remain in control and to create chaos and confusion in the family unit.

> *"Narcissists treat kids like little chess pieces in their ultimate game of "Who's in Control?, especially during a breakup. They'll happily use the kids to stir up drama and rewrite the story to make themselves the hero, completely ignoring the fact that their "master plan" might be turning the kids into emotional acrobats!"*

> *"Narcissist don't want a genuine relationship with their children; they want opportunity to use the child against you."*

Psychological impact on the child

Children subjected to narcissistic abuse often experience profound psychological impacts. They may become hypersensitive to remarks and judgments, constantly seeking validation yet feeling perpetually inadequate. This heightened sensitivity can lead to chronic anxiety and low self-esteem. In such toxic environments, children frequently grapple with confusion regarding parental affection. The manipulative tactics of the narcissistic parent can distort the child's perception, making it challenging to discern genuine love from manipulation. Consequently, they may feel unloved by both parents, leading to trust issues and emotional withdrawal.

This emotional turmoil can manifest in behaviors that resemble symptoms of neurodevelopmental disorders. While narcissistic abuse does not cause conditions like autism or ADHD, the chronic stress and trauma can lead to difficulties in attention, impulsivity, and social interactions, which may be misinterpreted as such disorders. It's crucial to differentiate between true neurodevelopmental disorders and trauma responses to ensure appropriate support and intervention. The manipulative behaviors of the narcissistic parent can erode the child's trust in both parents. The child may become ambivalent about living with either parent, unable to recognize genuine care due to the narcissistic parent's facade and brainwashing tactics.

On the flip side, children exposed to narcissistic abuse might also adopt narcissistic traits, either as a learned behavior or due to genetic predisposition. Growing up in an environment where manipulation, control, and dominance are modeled as the means to achieve goals can leave a profound imprint on a child's personality. The child may begin to emulate the narcissistic parent, seeing their behavior as effective and rewarding. They may view the other parent's perceived "weakness" or lack of authority as an opportunity to assert their own dominance, unknowingly mirroring the abusive dynamics they have witnessed. This behavior can provide the child with a temporary sense of power and control in an otherwise chaotic and emotionally unstable environment. However, what they fail to realize is that the narcissistic parent's approval and "love" are conditional. Eventually, the narcissistic parent may turn on them, subjecting them to the same patterns of manipulation and abuse.

This betrayal can create a deeply conflicted and wounded individual, caught between seeking validation from the abusive parent and grappling with the internalized behaviors they've adopted.

The cycle perpetuates a toxic legacy, underscoring the critical importance of intervention and support to help the child break free from these patterns and develop healthier ways of relating to others. Recognizing these dynamics early can prevent the transmission of narcissistic traits to future generations.

The Narcissist's Need for Power and Control

Even after the divorce is finalized, the narcissist's hunger for control doesn't end. They need a consistent supply of emotional fuel, and they'll design the divorce agreement to ensure they can keep making your life a living hell. Their ultimate goal is to subtly control you through your children, ensuring they remain the center of attention in your life, even if they are no longer physically present.

Their control is not just about maintaining power over you—it's about keeping you emotionally and psychologically bound. The narcissist will manipulate any agreement to continue extracting supply from you, all while offering nothing in return.

> *"Circular conversations are a manipulative tactics used by narcissists to evade accountability and maintain control by exhausting and confusing their victims."*

Inability to give a stable Family Life

Narcissists are incapable of providing a stable family life because their self-centered behavior extends to critical aspects like finances, children's education, and living conditions. They keep the family trapped in a cycle of uncertainty by prioritizing their needs and desires over the well-being of others. Here's how this plays out practically:

1. **Financial Instability**

   Narcissists often misuse family finances to exert control or boost their image, such as making impulsive purchases, overspending on luxuries, or refusing to contribute to household needs. They also withhold money as a form of control, leaving the family with insufficient resources for basic necessities like rent, utilities, or groceries. This creates financial stress and insecurity within the household.

2. **Neglecting Children's Education**

   A narcissist's lack of foresight and responsibility often impacts their children's education. They may refuse to pay school fees on time, make arbitrary decisions about schooling without consulting their partner, or deliberately disrupt the child's routine by prioritizing their own ego or conflicts. This can lead to gaps in the child's learning and emotional distress due to the instability.

3. **Poor Living Conditions**

   Maintaining a comfortable and safe home environment is rarely a priority for narcissists unless it benefits their public image. They may refuse to invest in necessary home repairs, neglect basic maintenance, or create a toxic household atmosphere through constant conflict and control. This leaves the family in substandard living conditions that affect their overall well-being.

4. **Constant Uncertainty**

   The narcissist's erratic behavior and lack of accountability mean the partner is often left guessing about their future. Will bills be paid? Will the child's school needs be met? Will the home be a place of peace or chaos today? This persistent unpredictability forces the partner into survival mode, unable to plan or grow in a healthy and stable environment.

Ultimately, the narcissist's need for control and self-gratification creates a volatile foundation for the family—depriving them of the security, structure, and consistency essential for a healthy life.

Survivor's Story:

Sarah had always known that Daniel was controlling, but she never imagined he would stoop down so low just to free himself of responsibility. Their marriage had been a battlefield where she had fought endlessly for stability, but the moment she tried to break free, the battle turned brutal.

Daniel was never going to let her go easily—not because he loved her, not because he cared for their child, but because control was his ultimate weapon. He didn't just want to win—**he wanted to ensure she lost everything.**

When coercion and manipulation failed, he turned to deception. He fabricated stories, twisted the truth, and played the victim flawlessly. He weaponized lies against her, and when words weren't enough, he escalated his tactics—calling the police, falsely accusing her of violence and abuse. The accusations were absurd, but they served their purpose.

His strategy was clear- to make Sarah so desperate that she would have no choice but to leave on his terms. He created an unbearable, hostile environment—one that put their child at risk. His ultimate goal was not just to drive them out, but to ensure they had no way back.

Daniel coerced Sarah into leaving the country, knowing that once she was gone, he could seal their fate. He had never wanted the child in the first place, and by forcing them out, he ensured they would never return. He wanted to live his life unburdened, free from any obligations—no child support, no alimony, no financial ties. This was never about losing his family—it was about protecting himself from having to pay for them.

Sarah on the other hand was only concerned about the child's future, she in fact stayed in the marriage so that the child's upbringing should not get impacted.

And so, when Sarah finally left—uprooting the life she had fought to build, Daniel made his next move. He twisted the narrative, filing a child abduction case against her. The very act he had orchestrated now became his weapon to cement himself as the victim. In one breath, he had pushed them out. In the next, he accused her of stealing the child away from him. That was the cruelty of narcissistic abuse—creating conflicting realities so that no matter what happened, he remained blameless.

Sarah and her child left behind everything they had built together; their home, their belongings, their memories. In a single day, their world was ripped away from them. The little girl had to leave her school materials, her clothes, her favorite things—everything that was once familiar and safe. And Sarah had to abandon the possessions she had worked so hard to earn through her own hustle and struggle, now left in Daniel's possession, serving as yet another reminder of all he had taken from them.

Even now, they still struggle. The weight of those memories lingers, creeping up in unexpected moments, bringing tears to their eyes. The pain of everything they lost—the life they had built, the dreams they had for the future remains a wound that never fully heals.

> *"She didn't want to move or speak. She wanted to rest, to learn, to dream. She felt very tired."- Virginia Woolf*

*Ladies and gentlemen, this is how you lose a battle to a narcissist. He will win. He will always win. He has always known he would win. Because narcissists have zero empathy. They don't care who they destroy, as long as they get what they want. To them, it's not about love, fairness, or justice—it's about **power**. It's a game. And in their game, you don't just lose. You are shattered— mentally, emotionally, physically, financially, and in ways you never imagined possible.*

> *"You can be in so much pain yet still unable to explain what you are experiencing to someone who has not experienced narcissistic abuse."*

The Psychological Impact of Divorce on a Child (Caught Between a Narcissistic and a Loving Parent)

Divorce is already a difficult experience for a child, but when one parent is a narcissist, the emotional toll becomes far more damaging. The child is caught in a silent war—a battle between a parent who truly loves them and a parent who seeks control at any cost.

A narcissistic parent doesn't just separate from their partner—they wage a psychological campaign to turn the child against the loving parent. They distort reality, weaponizing lies to create confusion and distrust. They paint the safe parent as the villain while presenting themselves as the only source of truth and security. The child, still developing emotionally and mentally, struggles to process these conflicting narratives.

The Emotional Confusion

Children rely on stability and consistency to develop a healthy sense of trust and self-worth. But under the influence of a narcissistic parent, stability is replaced with manipulation. The child begins to question their own feelings— *If one parent says they love me, but the other tells me that love is fake, who do I believe?* They become torn between loyalty to both parents, fearing the consequences of trusting the wrong one.

Living in Constant Fear

One of the most devastating effects of being trapped between a narcissistic and a loving parent is the ongoing fear of conflict. The child learns to anticipate tension, dreading the moment the narcissistic parent will escalate a situation, lash out, or create a scene. They watch helplessly as the narcissist launches verbal or emotional attacks on the safe parent, feeling powerless to stop it. The child driven by fear, feels compelled to demonstrate loyalty to the narcissistic parent to avoid the risk of having their basic needs withheld, an emotional weapon the narcissist uses to maintain control.

Over time, the child internalizes this fear and begins altering their own behavior to avoid triggering the narcissist's wrath. They develop a heightened sense of awareness, constantly scanning the environment for signs of an impending outburst. This hypervigilance forces them into survival mode learning to suppress their emotions, avoid certain topics, and act in ways that keep the narcissist appeased.

Walking on Eggshells and the False Persona

To cope with the unpredictable nature of the narcissistic parent, the child learns to wear a mask. They put up a false attitude in front of the narcissist, pretending to agree with them, acting cheerful when they feel anxious, and hiding any affection they have for the loving parent. They learn that showing independence, questioning the narcissist's version of events, or displaying sadness could provoke anger, punishment, or even withdrawal of love.

Walking on eggshells becomes second nature. The child may overly apologize, avoid expressing opinions, or downplay their emotions just to maintain peace. They quickly learn that their true self isn't safe in the presence of the narcissist, leading to a fragmented sense of identity.

The Child's Deep-Rooted Fear of Abandonment

A child caught in the crossfire of a narcissistic parent's manipulation often develops deep-seated abandonment issues. From an early age, they are conditioned to believe that love is conditional and it is given when they comply and stripped away when they show independence or align with the safe parent. The narcissistic parent's unpredictable moods, silent treatments, and sudden withdrawals of affection instill a constant fear of rejection.

The child begins to equate love with performance, feeling the need to earn attention rather than receiving it unconditionally. This emotional instability teaches them that relationships are fragile and that expressing their true thoughts or emotions might lead to being discarded. They may suppress their needs, mold their personality to please others, or develop anxious attachment styles, fearing that any misstep will push people away.

This fear of abandonment extends beyond childhood, affecting their future relationships. They may struggle with trust, develop people-pleasing tendencies, or tolerate toxic behaviors just to avoid being left behind. The wounds of being emotionally neglected and used as a pawn in the narcissistic parent's battle can leave them feeling unworthy of love, always bracing for the moment when someone they care about will walk away, just as they were once made to feel by the very person who was supposed to protect them.

The Long-Term Consequences

Without intervention, a child caught in this dynamic may carry unresolved trauma into adulthood. Their self-esteem is eroded by years of gaslighting and emotional instability. The wounds inflicted during this period don't just fade—they shape the way they perceive love, trust, and self-worth for years to come.

How the Safe Parent Can Counteract Alienation and Rebuild Trust

When a child is subjected to a narcissistic parent's manipulation, their safe parent plays a crucial role in counteracting this damage and helping the child regain emotional stability. Here are some ways to rebuild trust and provide a sense of security:

1. **Consistent Emotional Availability**
   The child needs to know that love is not conditional. The safe parent must provide a stable, predictable environment where the child feels heard, valued, and accepted no matter what. Responding with patience and warmth, even when the child expresses confusion or resistance, helps reinforce emotional safety.

2. **Validate Their Feelings**

   A child caught between two conflicting narratives will struggle with self-doubt. The safe parent should acknowledge their emotions and reassure them that their feelings are real and important. Phrases like *"I understand this is confusing for you"* or *"It's okay to feel upset, and I'm here for you"* can help them feel seen and heard.

3. **Avoid Badmouthing the Narcissistic Parent**

   While it may be tempting to expose the narcissistic parent's lies, doing so directly can backfire, making the child feel like they have to "choose" sides. Instead, focus on showing them through actions what real love, honesty, and respect look like. Provide truth in a way that helps them critically think rather than feel torn.

4. **Reinforce Reality Gently**

   A narcissistic parent thrives on distorting reality. The safe parent can help counter this by subtly reaffirming facts. If the child repeats false claims they've been fed, respond calmly with, **"I understand that's what you've been told, but here's what really happened..."** and let them process at their own pace.

5. **Teach Healthy Boundaries**

   The child must learn that love doesn't mean tolerating mistreatment. Encouraging them to recognize and assert their needs without fear of punishment helps rebuild their self-worth. Give them small choices to help them regain a sense of control, such as choosing what to eat or what activity to do together.

6. **Be Patient and Lead by Example**

   Healing takes time, especially when the child has been conditioned to distrust one parent. Continue to show up, be emotionally available, and model healthy communication and love. Even if the child pushes back or doubts your intentions, your consistent actions will eventually break through the narcissist's conditioning.

7. **Encourage Open Communication Without Pressure**
   The child may hesitate to share their true thoughts out of fear of upsetting the narcissistic parent. Create a safe space where they can express themselves without judgment. Avoid pressuring them to talk—instead, let them know you are always available when they're ready.

8. **Seek Professional Support**
   Therapy with a professional who understands narcissistic abuse can provide the child with tools to process their emotions and develop healthy coping mechanisms. If direct therapy isn't possible, engaging in books, activities, or discussions that promote emotional intelligence can be an alternative way to help.

By remaining a stable, loving force in the child's life, the safe parent can slowly undo the psychological damage caused by the narcissistic parent. Over time, the child will begin to see the contrast between manipulation and genuine care, allowing them to reconnect with the truth and build trust in healthy relationships.

Narcissist And The New Supply

A narcissist's need for a constant stream of validation and control drives them to seek out new sources of supply. The "new supply" is the next person they target, manipulate, and draw into their web of deceit. While this new person may feel special in the beginning, they are ultimately just another pawn in the narcissist's endless cycle of emotional exploitation.

Understanding the Narcissist's New Supply

In the world of narcissistic abuse, the term **"new supply"** refers to the next person a narcissist targets for validation, control and emotional exploitation. This new person often believes they've found a loving and attentive partner, only to later experience the same cycle of idealization, devaluation, and discard that previous victims endured.

The concept of narcissistic supply is fundamental to understanding why narcissists behave the way they do. Unlike emotionally healthy individuals who have a stable sense of self-worth, narcissists rely on external validation to feel important, admired, and in control. They require a constant **"supply"** of attention, praise, and emotional reactions from others to maintain their inflated self-image.

However, no single person can meet their insatiable need for validation forever. Over time, the **current supply** (victim) may start questioning their behavior, setting boundaries, or simply becoming emotionally drained from the abuse. At this point, the narcissist starts grooming or seeking **new supply**—a fresh target who is unaware of their toxic patterns and will provide them with the admiration and devotion they crave.

Why Narcissists Always Seek a New Source of Validation

1. **Narcissistic Supply is Their Lifeline**
   Narcissists don't have a stable, internal sense of self-worth. They rely entirely on external validation to prop up their fragile egos. When their current victim (or "supply") starts showing signs of independence, questioning their behavior, or no longer providing the same level of admiration, they begin seeking fresh sources of attention.

2. **The Thrill of the Chase**
   The beginning of any relationship is filled with excitement, admiration, and intense emotions. For narcissists, this honeymoon phase is intoxicating because they are showered with praise, trust, and adoration. Once this phase ends, they lose interest because maintaining a long-term connection requires emotional depth, vulnerability, and responsibility—things they are incapable of.

3. **Escaping Accountability**
   When a narcissist's mask starts slipping, their current partner might begin questioning their behavior or setting boundaries. Rather than

introspecting or changing, the narcissist preemptively seeks a new target who will see them as perfect. By doing this, they avoid being held accountable for their past mistreatment.

4. **Punishing the Old Supply**

Discarding their current partner for a new one serves another purpose—psychological punishment. Narcissists want their previous victim to feel rejected, worthless, and easily replaceable. They flaunt the new relationship to rub salt into the wound, making their ex question whether they were the problem all along.

5. **Maintaining a Backup Plan**

Many narcissists engage in parallel relationships, grooming new supply long before discarding the old one. This ensures they are never alone or without an emotional energy source. The moment they feel their current partner pulling away, they seamlessly transition to the next one without ever having to experience emotional emptiness.

After the Idealization: The New Supply's Reality

1. **From Worshipped to Worthless**

The new supply is initially put on a pedestal, just as all previous victims were. They are made to feel like they are the love of the narcissist's life—until reality sets in. Once the narcissist secures their emotional investment, they slowly begin to devalue them.

2. **The Subtle Undermining Begins**

After the love-bombing phase, the narcissist starts introducing small criticisms, subtle jabs, and moments of emotional withdrawal. The new supply, still high from the initial idealization, works harder to regain the narcissist's approval, unknowingly stepping into the cycle of abuse.

3. **Psychological Gaslighting and Control**
   The narcissist starts using gaslighting, triangulation, and emotional withholding to destabilize the new supply's self-worth. They might compare them to the ex, accuse them of overreacting, or suddenly become emotionally distant. The new supply, confused and desperate to restore the original affection, begins walking on eggshells.

4. **Public vs. Private Persona**
   The narcissist continues to present their new relationship as "perfect" to the outside world, especially on social media. Meanwhile, behind closed doors, the abuse escalates. The new supply starts realizing that the charming person they fell for is not the one they are actually in a relationship with.

5. **Testing Boundaries and Breaking Them**
   Narcissists push the limits of emotional, verbal and sometimes physical abuse. They gradually introduce more extreme forms of manipulation, seeing how much the new supply will tolerate. The more the supply forgives, the worse the abuse becomes.

6. **The Discard and Smear Campaign**
   Eventually, the narcissist either grows bored or the new supply starts resisting their control. This leads to the inevitable discard phase. The narcissist might abruptly leave them for yet another new supply or begin smearing them, portraying them as unstable, clingy, or even abusive.

7. **Hoovering and Reopening the Cycle**
   If the narcissist feels they can still extract something from the previous supply, they might reappear with apologies, fake remorse, or promises to change. The new supply, now psychologically broken, might fall for the illusion and the cycle begins again.

CHAPTER 8

NARCISSIST VS EMPATH

Narcissists often target empaths due to the complementary dynamics between their personalities. Empaths are naturally intuitive, compassionate, and inclined to prioritize others' needs, making them susceptible to the manipulative tactics of narcissists. This dynamic allows narcissists to exploit empaths' nurturing tendencies to fulfill their own desires for attention and control.

Interestingly, both narcissists and empaths may emerge from dysfunctional family backgrounds, sharing core wounds such as feelings of inadequacy or low self-worth. Despite these common origins, their responses diverge significantly.

- **Narcissists:** Often develop defense mechanisms characterized by self-centeredness and a lack of empathy, using manipulation to assert dominance and protect their fragile self-esteem.

- **Empaths:** Tend to become more attuned to others' emotions, striving to heal and support those around them, often at their own expense.

This contrast creates a compelling, albeit toxic, attraction between the two:

- **For Narcissists:** Conquering a strong, empathetic individual provides a sense of power and validation, as they take pleasure in breaking down someone with depth and resilience.

- **For Empaths:** Their innate desire to heal and understand others can lead them to tolerate and attempt to fix the narcissist's behavior, often to their own detriment.

This interplay underscores the complex and often damaging relationships that can form between narcissists and empaths, highlighting the importance of awareness and boundaries for empaths to protect their well-being.

Narcissists are indeed often highly intuitive and intelligent, particularly when it comes to reading people and situations. They possess a keen ability to assess **vulnerabilities**, adapt their behavior to manipulate others, and navigate social dynamics to their **advantage**. However, their intelligence is usually employed in self-serving and exploitative ways, aimed at controlling and dominating others rather than fostering genuine connection or growth. Narcissist clearly lack wisdom.

On the other hand, empaths not only possess emotional intelligence but also **wisdom**. Their wisdom comes from a deep understanding of emotions, compassion, and life experiences, allowing them to approach situations with a sense of purpose and moral clarity. Empaths use their insight to heal, uplift, and nurture those around them.

" Your empathy does not fix Narcissist"

The difference lies in how these traits are channeled:

- **Narcissists:** Intuition and intelligence are tools for manipulation. They lack the wisdom to value emotional depth, integrity, or the consequences of their actions on others. Instead, their focus is on immediate gratification, power, and maintaining their fragile self-image.

- **Empaths:** While also intuitive and emotionally intelligent, empaths possess the wisdom to use their abilities for positive impact. They value authenticity, connection, and growth—not just for themselves, but for others.

This fundamental distinction highlights why narcissists and empaths often become entangled. Narcissists exploit their intelligence for control, while empaths, driven by wisdom and compassion, strive to heal and understand— even at great personal cost.

"*Narcissist feeds on emptiness, while an empath seeks to heal the void*"

How Empaths Are Made:

Pain, especially from a traumatic childhood or overwhelming experiences, has a powerful way of pushing your energy upward, heightening your intuition and awareness. It makes you more attuned to others' emotions, patterns, and unresolved traumas. In this sense, pain is a gift, helping you grow and connect on a deeper level. However, this can be extremely overwhelming as you are hyper attuned to others emotional state and energies on the receiving end. Empaths develop a habit of self sabotaging and lack boundaries when it comes to helping and heal others. Empaths have exceptional pattern recognition. They have solid grasp on psychology and often explain your issues to you before you become aware of them.

"*A soul that carries empathy is a soul that has survived enormous pain*"

Some people awaken spiritually without ever coming into contact with any meditation technique or any spiritual teaching. They may awaken simply because they can't stand the suffering anymore. Empaths are such souls and they are highly intuitive. Intuition is a superpower and people who hear it know it is something mystical, knowing everything without even thinking is phenomenon beyond the mind. That's why people who haven't experienced it have a hard time believing it.

Empaths thrive in relationships rooted in honesty and open communication. At the same time, they also need space to be themselves and recharge their energy.

Empaths are highly intuitive, multi sensory, spiritually attune and acutely observant. They feel every emotion very deep to the highest degree and get easily overwhelmed if not grounded. They can sense the energy under the words, passive aggression, tension in the room, words not said and unspoken expectations.

Empaths are also very simple souls and draw joy out of very simple things. They are also very anxious beings as they can easy sense the energy of their surroundings. They are uncomfortable in the crowd or gatherings if they don't shield their energy. They are deeply connect with nature. Your emotional intelligence and intuition will offend everyone who can't manipulate them.

Unfortunately, empaths often encounter skepticism because many people cannot understand a pure soul and honest intentions. Having never experienced that kind of energy before, it feels foreign to them, making them unreceptive to it.

> *Empaths walk through two phases—naïve innocence and awakened strength. In the first, they love without limits, driven by people-pleasing and a deep fear of abandonment, making them easy prey for narcissists and manipulators. This cycle leads to devastating exploitation, shattering them entirely. Yet, from this destruction comes transformation—they rebuild with firm boundaries, self-respect, and emotional intelligence. No longer exploitable, they emerge as empowered empaths, wielding their kindness with intention, unstoppable in their strength.*

> *"I don't just listen to your words, I listen to your use of words, your tone, your body movements, your eyes, your subtle face expressions. I interpret your silences — I can hear everything you don't say"*

HSP- Highly Sensitive Person

A highly sensitive person (HSP) is a neurodivergent individual who is thought to have an increased or deeper central nervous system sensitivity to physical, emotional, or social stimuli. Some refer to this as having sensory processing sensitivity, or SPS for short. People born with SPS have increased sensitivity to central nervous system and deeper cognitive processing of physical, social and emotional stimuli. Apparently, only 15 to 20 percent of population is born with this gift.

HSPs are naturally introverted, intuitive, visionary and involved with their soul and spiritual life.

As per research, lack of parental warmth growing up may cause a child to develop high sensitivity and carry this trait into adulthood. The same goes for negative early childhood experiences. If you experienced trauma as a child, you may be more likely to become an HSP as an adult. Genetics may contribute to high sensitivity.

If you are highly sensitive you have knack on picking up on things others miss. You catch little changes in how people act, the real meaning behind their gestures, and you can tell when someone is being nice just for show. You can sense the energy of a person situation and a place. You can sense when someone has a sight shift in their energies.

HSPs may be more susceptible to being stressed by conflict. They may be more aware of trouble brewing in a relationship, including when things just feel a little off with someone who may not be communicating that there is a problem.

HSPs and empaths need to recharge daily. If they fail to do so, they will end up experiencing confusion anger, sensory overload, physical and emotional burn out and anxiety attacks.

> *"If you are sensitive, it's not something to "heal from" because it's not a wound or a flaw. Sensitivity is a profound gift; one that allows you to perceive the world deeply, feel intensely, and connect with nuance and truth. It's not about fixing it- it's about embracing and empowering it."*

Borderline Personality Disorder (BPD) vs Narcissistic Personality Disorder (NPD)

Borderline Personality Disorder (BPD) and Narcissistic Personality Disorder (NPD) share some similarities, primarily in how individuals with these disorders navigate their relationships and sense of self, though they manifest in different ways. Both conditions are rooted in deep insecurities, though the coping mechanisms and behaviors vary. A person with BPD often experiences intense emotional instability, an overwhelming fear of abandonment, and struggles with maintaining a consistent self-image. These emotional extremes can lead to frantic efforts to avoid real or imagined abandonment, which may trigger impulsive actions or self-destructive behaviors.

In contrast, individuals with NPD exhibit a grandiose sense of self-importance, a need for admiration, and a lack of empathy. Their sense of self is fragile, but instead of showing vulnerability like those with BPD, they overcompensate with arrogance and a desire to control others to maintain their inflated self-image. Both disorders can lead to destructive relationships, as individuals with BPD may become overly dependent or clingy, while those with NPD might manipulate, belittle, or exploit others to keep their sense of superiority intact.

Despite these differences, the core issue in both disorders is an underlying insecurity. People with BPD often feel emotionally empty, constantly searching for validation, while those with NPD need to feel superior and powerful to cover up their internal emptiness. Both may engage in dramatic, attention-seeking behaviors, though the motivations differ. For example, someone with BPD may engage in reckless actions to cope with perceived abandonment, while a narcissist might manipulate or exploit others to reinforce their superiority.

In relationships, both types struggle with emotional regulation, though they express it in different ways. While BPD tends to lead to emotional outbursts and an unstable sense of self, NPD's focus is on control, validation, and ensuring that others remain beneath them. The common thread between both conditions is that their emotional needs are unmet, leading them to use external sources—whether it's attention, admiration, or control to fill that void. This dynamic makes both disorders difficult to manage, particularly for those in relationships with them.

THE SILENT SUFFERING: UNDERSTANDING THE VICTIM'S TRAUMA

Narcissistic abuse is an invisible wound that lingers long after the abuse itself has ended. Unlike physical wounds, which are evident and acknowledged, the psychological scars of a victim are often dismissed, invalidated, or misunderstood. Victims live in a constant state of internal chaos—doubting their own experiences, questioning their reality, and struggling to articulate the depth of their suffering. Their body holds onto the trauma, responding to even minor stressors with panic, numbness, or exhaustion, as if the threat never truly ended. Invalidation, both from the narcissist and from those who fail to understand the abuse, further deepens the wound, making the victim feel unseen and unheard. This silent suffering, often dismissed as mere overreaction or sensitivity, is a direct consequence of prolonged psychological warfare- one that leaves victims struggling with anxiety, dissociation, and a fractured sense of self.

Invalidation received by the victims

"Secondary trauma happens when your story is heard by the wrong crowed and invalidated"

One of the most agonizing aspects of surviving narcissistic abuse is the overwhelming invalidation victims face whenever they attempt to share their story or seek support. Unlike physical abuse, which leaves visible wounds, narcissistic abuse is psychological, emotional, and often covert—making it incredibly difficult to explain to those who have never experienced it. This lack of tangible proof creates a devastating reality where victims are not only gaslit by their abuser but also dismissed, questioned, and misunderstood by society, legal systems, and even their closest friends and family.

When a survivor finally gathers the courage to open up about their experience, they are frequently met with skepticism. People struggle to comprehend how someone who appears so charming, successful, or "normal" could be capable of such cruelty behind closed doors. The abuser has spent years carefully curating their public image, ensuring that no one would believe their victim when the truth is finally revealed. Survivors often hear responses like, *"Are you sure you're not exaggerating?"*, *"He doesn't seem like that kind of person,"* or *"Maybe you're just being too sensitive."* These statements reinforce the narcissist's narrative, leaving the victim feeling unheard, dismissed, and questioning their own reality all over again.

> *There is a term called "dog whistling". A dog whistle is a whistle that only a dog can hear. Narcissists will do things in public or around a lot of people that they know will bother you. But everyone else is immune to what they are doing. They will do offensive things in a way that no one expects you know the context to which they are meaning it. It will appear innocent to everyone else. If you react to it, everyone thinks you are the only one that is out of line. The narcissist plays innocent, and you appear to be the unreasonable one.*

Family and Friends Seeing You Through an Outdated Lense

Judged by your past: Family members, in particular, may still see you through the lens of your childhood or earlier years, holding onto outdated perceptions of you. If you made mistakes or had challenges in the past, those experiences might be used to discredit your present reality. The fact that narcissists thrive on exploiting these perceptions adds to the difficulty. They subtly (or sometimes not-so-subtly) reinforce the idea that you're the one with problems, while they remain calm and composed.

Difficulty breaking old patterns: It's challenging to convince those closest to you, like **family**, to see beyond those old patterns, especially when they have no direct experience of the narcissist's abusive behavior. Family dynamics can play a huge role in how the situation is perceived, often leading to invalidation of the survivor's feelings.

The legal system, often manipulated by narcissists, may fail to recognize the abuser's deceptive tactics, forcing victims to relive their trauma in court while their abuser plays the victim flawlessly. Even within support circles, survivors may find themselves compared to others with "worse" experiences, as if their suffering is not valid enough to warrant help.

This level of invalidation deepens the emotional wounds inflicted by the narcissist. After years of being gaslit and having their feelings disregarded, victims desperately seek validation from the outside world, only to be met with more dismissal. It reinforces the abuser's conditioning; *that no one will believe them, that they are alone, and that maybe they are the problem. Many survivors end up retreating into silence, feeling more isolated than ever, because the pain of not being believed becomes just as unbearable as the abuse itself.*

The emotional toll of this invalidation is profound. Victims struggle with self-doubt, shame, and a sense of invisibility, making it harder to heal and rebuild their lives. The fear of judgment prevents many from seeking justice or leaving the relationship sooner. For some, the silence becomes a survival mechanism—they stop speaking about their pain altogether, internalizing their trauma, and suffering in isolation.

For female victims, especially those who are financially dependent on their abuser, the invalidation is even more severe. Society's ingrained male chauvinism conditions people to believe that a woman must stay with her husband, regardless of the abuse she endures. The belief that a man has the right to exercise control over his wife; financially, emotionally, and even psychologically—is so deeply embedded that when a woman dares to stand up for herself, society punishes her with further invalidation. Instead of offering help, people doubt her story, assuming she must be exaggerating or fabricating the abuse. The truth is uncomfortable, and rather than confronting it, many prefer to dismiss it entirely.

> *"Empathy and support should be universal and not influenced by the gender. Addressing abuse means standing against injustice, and not against any specific gender. Supporting or enabling an abuser makes one equally responsible for the abuse."*

Invalidation also comes from **professionals** who are meant to provide support. Therapists unfamiliar with narcissistic abuse may minimize the victim's suffering, offering generic advice like *"Have you tried talking things out?"* or *"Maybe you both have issues to work on"* Narcissists are master manipulators, skilled at presenting themselves as charming, reasonable, and even victimized. In therapy, they wear their mask so well that the counselor, unaware of the covert abuse, may end up siding with the abuser. The victim, already struggling to articulate their trauma, is thrown under the bus as the narcissist skillfully shifts blame, portraying them as unstable, overly emotional, or even abusive. This reversal of roles can be devastating, leaving the victim feeling completely defeated, as even the professionals meant to help fail to see the truth.

The invalidation that victims face; whether from loved ones, society, or professionals; creates a second layer of trauma that can be just as damaging as the abuse itself. It forces victims into silence, making them question their own experiences and keeping them trapped in a cycle of suffering. The lack of support is not just disheartening—it actively enables the abuser, allowing them to continue their manipulation unchecked. What survivors need most is validation—someone who listens, understands, and acknowledges their reality. But in a world conditioned to protect the abuser and doubt the victim, that validation is heartbreakingly rare.

> *"Psychological invalidation is one of the most lethal forms of emotional abuse. It kills confidence, creativity and individuality."*

> *"People who have not experienced narcissistic abuse have no idea what strength it takes to survive. These people will be dismissive and*

label you as untruthful, neurotic and unstable. Narcissistic abuse is so extreme and cruel that it seems to be fabricated to those who have not experienced it."- Jill wise

"Trauma doesn't come from merely the hurt. It comes from becoming entangled with someone who has malevolent intentions to break you"- Jordan Peterson

How Trauma Affects the Brain

Trauma leaves an imprint on the brain, particularly in areas responsible for fear, memory, and emotional regulation. The amygdala, the brain's fear center becomes hyperactive, leading to an exaggerated response to stress and perceived threats. This heightened sensitivity makes trauma survivors more prone to anxiety, hypervigilance, and emotional reactivity. The hippocampus, which is responsible for processing memories, may shrink in response to prolonged trauma, impairing the ability to differentiate between past and present danger. This is why trauma survivors often experience flashbacks, where their body reacts as though they are reliving a past traumatic event.

Additionally, trauma alters the function of the prefrontal cortex, the part of the brain responsible for rational thinking and decision-making. When trauma is severe, this area struggles to regulate emotions effectively, leading to impulsive reactions, difficulty concentrating, and an inability to feel a sense of safety, even in non-threatening environments. The victim may feel constantly on edge, unable to trust their surroundings, and overwhelmed by emotions they cannot control. The amygdala becomes overactive due to ongoing distress.

"What doesn't kill you sometimes makes you wish it did, dysregulates your nervous system, steals your identity and destroys your sense of security. Stop glorifying trauma." - Amanda Webster

Psychological Impact on Victims

Narcissistic abuse trauma runs deep, yet awareness of its effects remain limited. Victims often feel a profound internal change but struggle to pinpoint it. Many realizations come to light only after escaping the narcissist's control and leaving survival mode.

This trauma disrupts brain function, leading to memory loss, brain fog, and difficulty processing information. Victims frequently feel mentally overwhelmed by noise and conflict, and trust issues can keep them trapped in a cycle of survival. They may also experience changes in speech and communication, and their personalities may shift significantly.

Physically, victims often develop ailments like autoimmune diseases and gut issues due to suppressed emotions and chronic stress. A constant state of fight or flight weakens the immune system and disrupts gut health, resulting in chronic inflammation, digestive issues, and unexplained pain.

What is Trauma?

Trauma is a deeply distressing or disturbing experience that overwhelms an individual's ability to cope, leaving lasting psychological and physiological effects. It is not just a memory of an event but a fundamental rewiring of the brain and nervous system in response to overwhelming fear, helplessness, or prolonged exposure to stress. Trauma is often misunderstood as a single catastrophic event, such as an accident or natural disaster, but it can also be insidious, stemming from prolonged emotional and psychological distress. Trauma can result from experiences of intense fear, helplessness, or horror, particularly when a person feels trapped or powerless.

At its core, trauma is the body's response to a perceived threat that exceeds its ability to process or escape. When a person experiences trauma, their brain activates survival mechanisms designed to protect them. However, when the distressing experience is ongoing or repeated, as in cases of chronic emotional abuse or neglect, the body remains in a prolonged state of high alert, unable to return to a state of safety. This constant activation of the stress response alters the way the brain processes emotions, stores memories, and perceives the world, leading to long-term consequences that shape the victim's entire psychological and physical well-being.

Trauma in narcissistic abuse

Trauma from narcissistic abuse is not just the result of singular acts of cruelty—it is the accumulation of psychological wounds inflicted over time. Unlike overt physical violence, which leaves visible scars, this form of trauma operates in the shadows, embedding itself deep into the victim's psyche. The abuse is often subtle, laced with gaslighting, silent treatments, intermittent affection, and strategic invalidation, making the victim doubt their own experiences. This creates an emotional prison where fear, confusion, and dependency replace rational thought. In the case of narcissistic abuse the victim is subjected to ongoing psychological violence which creates an environment that is ripe for trauma to take root.

One of the most devastating impacts is emotional dysregulation—victims are conditioned to exist in a heightened state of anxiety, never knowing when the next emotional attack will come. This constant hypervigilance rewires the brain, keeping the nervous system in a prolonged state of fight-or-flight. Over time, the body and mind become exhausted, making it difficult to distinguish safety from danger, love from manipulation.

Another key aspect is identity erosion. Narcissistic abusers systematically strip away a victim's sense of self. Through relentless criticism, undermining, and belittling, they make the victim feel incapable, incompetent, and unworthy of love or success. The survivor, once confident and self-assured, now questions every decision and action, fearing they will never be good enough. They may even internalize the abuser's false narrative, believing they are the problem, which deepens the trauma and keeps them trapped in the cycle.

A profound sense of isolation also takes root. The narcissist ensures that the victim becomes dependent on them by cutting them off from external support systems. Friends and family may be pushed away through manipulation, or the victim, too ashamed to admit what is happening, may withdraw on their own. This isolation amplifies feelings of helplessness and makes escape feel impossible, reinforcing the idea that the abuser is their only source of stability—even if that stability is built on chaos.

"The most difficult part in narcissistic abuse is to articulate your trauma to someone– unable to explain as to what your body and mind is going through. Its not the lack of words it's the confusion that's difficult to put into words."

Impact on Nervous System

Survival Mode

Survival mode is a state of nervous system dysregulation (The nervous system includes the brain, spinal cord, and a complex network of nerves) caused by prolonged stress. It occurs when the balance between the sympathetic nervous system (which triggers the fight-or-flight response) and the parasympathetic nervous system (which promotes rest and recovery) is disrupted.

The sympathetic nervous system acts like an accelerator, increasing heart rate, blood pressure and alertness to respond to threats. In contrast, the parasympathetic nervous system functions as a brake, helping the body relax after stress. When one system remains overactive for an extended period, the body stays stuck in survival mode.

This can manifest as anxiety and hypervigilance when the sympathetic nervous system dominates, keeping a person in a constant state of fight or flight. On the other hand, when the parasympathetic nervous system is overactive, it may lead to exhaustion, numbness, and depression. In both cases, the nervous system remains dysregulated, preventing the body from returning to a state of balance.

"Trauma doesn't make you stronger. It wreaks havoc on your nervous system. It hijacks your digestive track. It keeps you stuck in a loop of hyper vigilance. To suggest someone is stronger because of it, is to dismiss what they've had to do to survive."- Nate Postlethwait

If you're feeling overwhelmed, exhausted, or disconnected, your body may be stuck in survival mode. Here are some common signs:

- Skipping meals or forgetting to eat

- Constant worrying and racing thoughts

- Mental and physical exhaustion

- Difficulty remembering things, especially short-term

- Feeling emotionally numb or wanting to escape

- Trouble sleeping or experiencing restless nights

- Overeating or losing your appetite entirely

- Staring off into space, feeling dissociated

- Shallow, rapid breathing

- Struggling with motivation and focus

- Feeling easily overwhelmed and on edge

- Dizziness, lightheadedness, or a racing heart

- A constant sense of urgency, as if you're always behind

- Difficulty planning ahead or delegating tasks

- Struggling to make even simple decisions

- Mood swings or feeling unusually irritable

- A sense of detachment, as if nothing really matters

Survival mode looks different for everyone—some feel constantly wired and anxious, while others experience deep exhaustion and detachment. If several of these resonate with you, your nervous system may be stuck in survival mode, keeping you in a state of stress and self-preservation.

The Nervous System's Response to Trauma

The nervous system plays a critical role in trauma responses. When faced with a threat, the autonomic nervous system activates the fight, flight, freeze, or fawn responses, depending on the situation. In acute trauma, this response helps a person survive immediate danger. However, in chronic trauma, the nervous system remains dysregulated, leading to lasting consequences.

1. **Fight or Flight** – When trauma activates this response, the body is flooded with stress hormones like adrenaline and cortisol, preparing it to either confront the danger or escape. However, when trauma is ongoing, these stress hormones remain elevated, causing chronic anxiety, restlessness, insomnia, and even physical symptoms like heart palpitations and digestive issues.

2. **Freeze** – Some victims become paralyzed in response to trauma, unable to take action or express their emotions. This leads to dissociation, emotional numbness, and a sense of detachment from reality. In severe cases, victims may feel as though they are observing their life from the outside, disconnected from their own experiences.

3. **Fawn** – A lesser-known response to trauma is fawning, where the victim attempts to appease or accommodate their abuser in an effort to prevent further harm. This can lead to people-pleasing behaviors, an inability to assert boundaries, and difficulty recognizing one's own needs.

Over time, repeated trauma can keep the nervous system stuck in these states, making it difficult for the victim to regulate emotions, feel safe, or function in daily life.

PTSD and C-PTSD

Trauma leaves a lasting imprint on the mind and body, often leading to **Post-Traumatic Stress Disorder (PTSD)** or **Complex Post-Traumatic Stress**

Disorder (C-PTSD). These conditions develop when a person experiences overwhelming distress that the brain is unable to process or escape from, leaving them stuck in a state of psychological and physiological dysregulation. While both PTSD and C-PTSD stem from traumatic experiences, they differ in their causes, symptoms, and long-term effects.

Have you ever been triggered by something that shouldn't bother you— like a certain tone of voice, a specific place, or even a song? One moment, you're fine. The next, your heart is racing, your hands are shaky, and it feels like you're right back in the nightmare you thought you escaped. You know you're safe, but your body doesn't believe it. That's PTSD (Post-Traumatic Stress Disorder) and CPTSD (Complex PTSD) after narcissistic abuse.

Post-Traumatic Stress Disorder (PTSD)

PTSD is a severe anxiety disorder that develops after experiencing or witnessing a traumatic event. It is commonly associated with single-incident traumas such as **car accidents, natural disasters, sexual assault, or military combat.** The brain perceives the trauma as an ongoing threat, and the nervous system remains in a heightened state of alertness long after the danger has passed.

One of the defining characteristics of PTSD is **re-experiencing the trauma through flashbacks, nightmares, and intrusive thoughts.** The brain struggles to process the traumatic memory, causing it to resurface involuntarily in vivid and distressing ways. These memories feel as though the trauma is happening again in real time, making it difficult for the survivor to distinguish between past and present danger.

PTSD also leads to **hypervigilance, emotional numbness, avoidance behaviors, and difficulty regulating emotions.** Victims may go to great lengths to avoid anything that reminds them of the trauma, whether it's a place, a person, or a particular situation. This avoidance reinforces isolation and often leads to depression, anxiety, and difficulty maintaining relationships.

Complex Post-Traumatic Stress Disorder (C-PTSD)

While PTSD is often linked to **a single traumatic event**, C-PTSD arises from **prolonged and repeated trauma, especially when there is no escape or relief.** It is commonly seen in survivors of **childhood abuse, domestic violence, prolonged emotional neglect, captivity, or any situation where the victim is under ongoing control or manipulation.**

C-PTSD includes all the symptoms of PTSD but is much more complex due to the prolonged nature of the trauma. Victims of C-PTSD often experience **emotional dysregulation, deep-seated shame, distorted self-perception, and difficulties in forming and maintaining relationships.** The trauma is not just a memory—it becomes embedded in the victim's identity, shaping their beliefs about themselves and the world.

One of the hallmarks of C-PTSD is **emotional flashbacks.** Unlike PTSD flashbacks, which involve vivid reliving of a specific event, emotional flashbacks are **intense feelings of fear, helplessness, or shame that arise without a clear memory trigger.** A person may suddenly feel as though they are in danger, even when there is no actual threat, because their nervous system is still reacting as though the trauma is ongoing.

Another key feature of C-PTSD is **a distorted sense of self.** Victims often develop **deep-seated shame, guilt, or a belief that they are unworthy of love and care.** This is because prolonged trauma, especially when inflicted by caregivers or intimate partners, conditions the victim to believe they deserve the mistreatment. The abuser's constant invalidation and gaslighting make it difficult for the victim to trust their own emotions and perceptions.

Unlike PTSD, which primarily focuses on **fear-based reactions to trauma,** C-PTSD affects the **entire personality, emotional regulation, and interpersonal relationships.** It leads to difficulties in **forming trust, establishing boundaries, and feeling safe in any environment.** Many survivors of C-PTSD struggle with **chronic self-doubt, identity confusion, dissociation, and deep feelings of loneliness.**

The Long-Term Effects of PTSD and C-PTSD

Both PTSD and C-PTSD **rewire the brain, affecting the way victims process emotions, interact with others, and respond to stress.** The **amygdala,** which processes fear, becomes hyperactive, leading to an exaggerated startle response and persistent feelings of threat. The **hippocampus,** responsible for distinguishing between past and present danger, becomes impaired, making it difficult to move on from traumatic memories. The **prefrontal cortex,** responsible for rational thinking and emotional regulation, weakens, leading to impulsive reactions, difficulty calming down, and struggles with decision-making.

On a psychological level, PTSD and C-PTSD cause **chronic anxiety, depression, self-destructive behaviors, and dissociation.** Many survivors experience **suicidal thoughts, substance abuse issues, or engage in self-harm** as a way to escape emotional pain. The deep-rooted trauma also leads to difficulties in relationships, as survivors may either **avoid closeness due to fear of being hurt** or **cling to toxic dynamics that feel familiar due to past abuse.**

C-PTSD is particularly damaging because **it reshapes a person's entire worldview.** Survivors often feel permanently broken, unable to trust, and disconnected from themselves and others. They may struggle with **identity issues, difficulty experiencing joy, and an overwhelming sense of hopelessness.**

Physical Symptoms of PTSD and CPTSD

- **Chronic Fatigue** – The body remains in a constant state of stress, leading to persistent exhaustion even after rest.

- **Muscle Tension and Pain** – Ongoing activation of the fight-or-flight response results in stiffness, aches, and tension headaches.

- **Gastrointestinal Issues**- Stress and elevated cortisol levels can cause gut problems such as irritable bowel syndrome (IBS), bloating, nausea, acid reflux, and constipation.

- **Autoimmune Disorders** – Long-term stress weakens the immune system, increasing inflammation and triggering autoimmune responses.

- **High Cortisol and Adrenal Fatigue** – Prolonged stress keeps the body's cortisol levels elevated, leading to burnout and hormonal imbalances.

- **Sleep Disturbances** – Insomnia, vivid nightmares, and restless sleep can occur due to hypervigilance and dysregulation of the nervous system.

- **Frequent Illness Cardiovascular Issues**- Prolonged stress can result in an increased heart rate, high blood pressure, and palpitations.

- **Dizziness and Light-headedness** – An imbalance in the nervous system can affect blood pressure regulation, leading to dizziness.

- **Temperature Dysregulation** – Individuals may feel excessively hot or cold due to dysfunction in the autonomic nervous system.

- **Frequent Illness**– A weakened immune system can result in frequent colds, infections, or slow healing.

- **Skin Conditions**– Stress can trigger skin issues such as eczema, psoriasis, hives, or unexplained rashes.

These physical symptoms arise from the body being stuck in survival mode for an extended period. The prolonged fight-or-flight response disrupts normal bodily functions, making recovery from narcissistic abuse a journey that involves both emotional and physical healing.

Healing from PTSD and C-PTSD

Healing from trauma is a long and complex journey, but **it is possible.** Recovery involves **rebuilding a sense of safety, learning to regulate emotions, and breaking free from self-destructive patterns.** Trauma therapy, such as **EMDR (Eye Movement Desensitization and Reprocessing), somatic therapy, cognitive behavioral therapy (CBT), and dialectical behavior therapy (DBT),** can help reprocess traumatic memories and rewire the brain.

For C-PTSD survivors, healing also involves **reconstructing their sense of self, learning to trust their emotions, and breaking free from toxic**

conditioning. Support systems, safe relationships, and self-compassion play crucial roles in the recovery process.

PTSD and C-PTSD are not just conditions; they are **evidence of survival.** They are the brain and body's way of adapting to extreme stress, but with the right support and coping mechanisms, victims can regain control over their lives and move toward healing.

Anxiety and Depression

Anxiety and depression are not just emotional struggles—they are psychological conditions rooted in prolonged stress and trauma, particularly in survivors of narcissistic abuse. The persistent fear, emotional exhaustion, and deep sadness that follow such abuse can escalate into hopelessness, suicidal thoughts, and self-harm. To understand why this happens, it is crucial to examine how narcissistic abuse affects the brain, emotions, and overall mental health.

Both anxiety and depression significantly impact cognitive, emotional, and physiological functioning. Anxiety is marked by excessive worry, hypervigilance, and a persistent sense of impending danger, while depression manifests as hopelessness, emotional numbness, and an inability to experience pleasure (anhedonia). These conditions disrupt the brain's neurotransmitter systems—particularly serotonin, dopamine, and norepinephrine—which regulate mood, motivation, and stress responses. The prolonged stress caused by narcissistic abuse alters these systems, leaving survivors trapped in a cycle of fear, despair and emotional dysregulation.

Anxiety in Narcissistic Abuse

Have you ever felt on edge, like something bad is about to happen, even when everything seems fine? Maybe your heart starts racing when your phone rings, or you second-guess every text you send. You're exhausted, but your mind won't stop replaying conversations, wondering if you said or did something wrong; that's anxiety—but after narcissistic abuse, it's not just worry. It's survival mode that never fully switches off.

When you were in the relationship with a Narc, your body adapted to constant emotional landmines. You never knew what would set them off—the silent treatment, a sudden rage, or a guilt trip that made you question your own reality. Over time, your brain learned to stay hyper-alert, scanning for danger, even when there wasn't any. This is why, even after leaving, you still feel the weight of fear and self-doubt.

Think of it like a fire alarm that's been jammed on high. At first, it saved you, helped you navigate the abuse, avoid confrontation and protect yourself. But now even in a safe space, it keeps blaring at every small trigger. A certain tone of voice, a look, or even a familiar place can send your body into panic mode. That's anxiety after narcissistic abuse—your nervous system still preparing for a threat that no longer exists.

Anxiety in survivors stems from the constant state of hypervigilance they develop while dealing with the narcissist's unpredictable behavior. Survivors experience:

- **Excessive worry and fear** —Walking on eggshells, afraid of triggering the narcissist's rage or silent treatment.

- **Hypervigilance**—Always on edge, anticipating the next attack, accusation, or manipulation.

- **Intrusive thoughts and rumination**—Overanalyzing conversations, second-guessing reality due to gaslighting.

- **Physical symptoms**—Racing heart, muscle tension, digestive issues, and insomnia due to chronic stress.

- **People-pleasing and fawning response**—Over-apologizing or trying to fix situations to avoid further emotional harm.

This heightened state of alertness **rewires the brain's stress response**, leading to long-term dysregulation of the **amygdala (fear center)** and **prefrontal**

cortex (decision-making, rational thinking), making it harder for survivors to relax or trust themselves.

Depression in Narcissistic Abuse

Have you ever felt like the world would be better off without you? Like no matter how hard you try, nothing ever changes, and maybe—just maybe, it would be easier to just disappear? If you've had these thoughts, you're not alone. Depression after narcissistic abuse isn't just sadness or exhaustion—it can feel like drowning in hopelessness, where even breathing feels like too much effort.

Narcissistic abuse doesn't just break your heart—it rewires your mind. The constant gaslighting, invalidation, and emotional manipulation leave deep scars. Over time, you start believing the narcissist's lies—that you're worthless, unlovable, ugly or a burden. Even after leaving, those words echo in your head, making it hard to see your own value. And when the pain feels unbearable, the thought of escape can creep in—not because you want to die, but because you just want the suffering to stop.

Think of it like being trapped in a pitch-black tunnel. The narcissist took away your sense of self, your joy, and maybe even your will to fight. You feel stuck, convinced that there's no way out. Depression convinces you that the darkness is endless, that no one understands, and that nothing will ever get better. But here's what depression doesn't tell you—the tunnel isn't endless. There is a way out, even if you can't see it right now.

> *If you're struggling with thoughts of self-harm or suicide, please know this—Your mind is lying to you. You are not a burden. You are not weak. You are not beyond help. Depression after narcissistic abuse is your body's response to prolonged emotional trauma. It's not who you are—it's what you're experiencing.* **And just like the abuse wasn't your fault, these feelings aren't either.**

Depression in survivors develops from prolonged **emotional exhaustion, learned helplessness, and the constant cycle of devaluation and discard.** Survivors experience:

- **Feelings of worthlessness and self-doubt** – After being repeatedly told they are "not enough" or "too much."

- **Emotional numbness and detachment** – Losing interest in things they once enjoyed due to constant invalidation.

- **Chronic fatigue and low motivation** – Feeling drained after years of emotional warfare.

- **Suicidal thoughts and self-harm** – When hopelessness reaches a peak and they feel there is no escape.

- **Difficulty making decisions** – Fear of getting it wrong due to years of being controlled or criticized.

Narcissistic abuse **depletes the brain's neurotransmitters** (serotonin, dopamine, norepinephrine), leading to mood dysregulation, lack of pleasure (anhedonia), and an inability to see a hopeful future.

Panic Attacks After Narcissistic Abuse

Have you ever felt like your body is betraying you? Like out of nowhere, your heart starts pounding, your chest tightens, and you can't breathe—like you're about to die? Maybe it happens when you see their name pop up, hear a certain tone of voice or even for no clear reason at all—that's a panic attack. And after narcissistic abuse it's not just fear, it's your nervous system stuck in survival mode, reacting to threats that aren't there anymore.

Living with a narcissist meant constantly walking on a tightrope, never knowing when the next explosion, silent treatment, or manipulation would come. Your body learned to expect danger at every turn. Even after escaping, that internal alarm system doesn't shut off. Instead, it malfunctions, setting off full-blown panic attacks over the smallest reminders. Your body thinks it's protecting you, but instead, it's trapping you in a cycle of fear.

Think of it like a car alarm that keeps going off even when there's no break-in. Your nervous system got wired to react to chaos, so now, even a minor trigger like a sudden noise, a familiar scent, or even silence, can send you spiraling into full-blown panic. Your body floods with adrenaline, preparing to fight or flee, but there's no actual threat. It's terrifying, overwhelming, and exhausting, making you feel powerless in your own skin.

Panic attacks in survivors stem from the trauma response deeply embedded during narcissistic abuse. They experience:

- **Sudden, intense fear** – Feeling like something terrible is about to happen, even in safe environments.

- **Physical symptoms** – Rapid heartbeat, shortness of breath, dizziness, sweating, and chest pain that mimic a heart attack.

- **Derealization and depersonalization** – Feeling detached from reality, like you're watching yourself from the outside.

- **Uncontrollable shaking and numbness** – As the body releases a surge of stress hormones, making movement difficult.

- **Fear of losing control or going crazy** – The overwhelming sensation that you are powerless to stop the attack.

These episodes happen because the brain's fear center (the amygdala) is overactivated due to prolonged trauma, causing exaggerated stress responses even when no actual danger exists. Survivors often avoid certain places, people, or situations, fearing another attack which can lead to isolation and further emotional distress.

Cognitive Dissonance

Cognitive dissonance is the mental discomfort that results from holding two conflicting beliefs, values or attitudes. People tend to seek consistency in their attitudes and perceptions, so this conflict causes unpleasant feelings of unease or discomfort.

Cognitive Dissonance in Narcissistic Abuse

Have you ever felt like you're stuck between two completely different realities? One moment, you remember the narcissist's cruelty—the lies, the manipulation, the way they made you feel small. But then, another thought creeps in—Maybe it wasn't that bad. Maybe I overreacted. They did love me... right? Suddenly, you're questioning everything. That mental tug-of-war? That's cognitive dissonance.

Cognitive dissonance is what happens when two conflicting beliefs fight for space in your mind. It's that unsettling feeling when your heart says one thing, but your brain says another. You know they were toxic. You know they hurt you. But at the same time, there were good moments—times they made you feel special, like you were the center of their world. So which version is real? The abuser who made you cry or the one who held you close afterward and said they loved you?

Think of it like holding a hot and cold object in each hand. One burns, the other soothes. But because they exist at the same time, your brain doesn't know which sensation to trust. That's what narcissistic abuse does—it keeps you swinging between pain and false hope until you're too mentally exhausted to tell reality from illusion.

This confusion isn't an accident—it's a strategy. The narcissist fed you just enough kindness to keep you attached and just enough cruelty to keep you doubting yourself. If they were always horrible, leaving would be easy. If they were always loving, you wouldn't have suffered. But because they constantly switched between both, your mind struggles to reconcile the truth.

And here's the hardest part: Your brain wants to choose the version that hurts less. It's painful to accept that someone you trusted was manipulating you. It's easier to believe they just "made mistakes" or that you could have done something differently to make them stay kind. That's why breaking free from a narcissist isn't just about leaving—it's about rewiring your mind to accept the truth, even when it hurts.

If you're stuck in this mental battle, remind yourself—***The love was a lie. The abuse was real***. Every time you catch yourself romanticizing the past, bring yourself back to reality. Journal the painful moments. Read about narcissistic patterns. Talk to someone who can remind you what you went through. Because the moment you stop excusing their behavior, the fog starts to lift and that's when true healing begins.

Cognitive dissonance can be subtle and difficult to recognize, but certain feelings and behaviors may indicate its presence. Some common signs include:

- A sense of discomfort before making a decision or taking action.

- Attempting to justify or rationalize a choice or behavior after the fact.

- Feeling embarrassed or ashamed about an action and wanting to keep it hidden.

- Experiencing guilt or regret over something done in the past.

- Engaging in activities due to social pressure or fear of missing out (FOMO), even when they don't align with personal desires.

Low Self-Esteem/ People Pleasing

Low self-esteem is when someone lacks confidence about who they are and what they can do. They often feel incompetent, unloved, or inadequate. People who struggle with low self-esteem are consistently afraid about making mistakes or letting other people down. Typically, a person with low self-esteem—Is extremely critical of themselves. Downplays or ignores their positive qualities. Judges themselves to be inferior to their peers. Uses negative words to describe themselves such as stupid, fat, ugly or unlovable.

Low Self-Esteem & People-Pleasing in Narcissistic Abuse:

Have you ever apologized for something that wasn't your fault? Or felt guilty for saying NO, even when you had every right to? Maybe you find yourself bending over backward to keep others happy, afraid that if you don't, they'll leave or worse, get angry. If this sounds familiar, you're not just being "too nice." **You've been conditioned to believe that your worth depends on how well you serve others.**

Narcissistic abuse doesn't just break your confidence—it reprograms your entire sense of self. Over time, you learned that your needs didn't matter. Every time you tried to stand up for yourself, the narcissist made you feel selfish, ungrateful, or "too much." If you expressed hurt, they dismissed it. If you set a boundary, they pushed back harder. And so, to survive, you became the peacekeeper, the fixer, the giver, the one who never causes trouble.

Think of it like being a puppet on invisible strings. The narcissist pulled them, and you danced- learning that love had to be earned, that your worth depended on how useful you were. Even after leaving, those strings remain, controlling how you interact with the world. You say yes when you want to say no. You feel responsible for other people's emotions. **You shrink yourself to avoid upsetting anyone.**

This is why, after narcissistic abuse, simple acts of self-care like resting, setting boundaries, or putting yourself first feel wrong. Your brain has been wired to believe that if you stop giving, people will abandon you. But here's the truth: Healthy relationships don't require you to sacrifice yourself. **Real relationship doesn't come with the price tag of self-betrayal.**

Survivors often struggle with self-doubt, self-criticism, and a diminished sense of identity. Here are common signs:

1. **Constant Self-Doubt**

   o Second-guessing decisions, even small ones.

   o Seeking reassurance from others to feel validated.

   o Feeling incapable of making choices without external input.

2. **Negative Self-Talk**

   o   Frequent thoughts of **"I'm not good enough"** or **"I always mess up."**

   o   Internalizing the abuser's criticism as personal truth.

   o   Struggling to accept compliments, believing they are undeserved.

3. **Fear of Failure & Perfectionism**

   o   Avoiding new experiences due to fear of making mistakes.

   o   Overworking or over-preparing to avoid criticism.

   o   Feeling worthless if things don't go perfectly.

4. **People-Pleasing Behavior**

   o   Struggling to say "no" and setting poor boundaries.

   o   Prioritizing others' needs over personal well-being.

   o   Feeling guilty when asserting personal wants or needs.

5. **Shame & Guilt**

   o   Feeling unworthy of happiness or success.

   o   Blaming oneself for the abuse rather than recognizing the manipulator's role.

   o   Apologizing excessively, even when not at fault.

6. **Avoidance of Social Interactions**

   o   Withdrawing from relationships due to fear of judgment.

   o   Feeling undeserving of love, friendship, or kindness.

   o   Assuming others will reject or abandon them.

7. Tolerating Toxic Relationships

- Attracting or staying in unhealthy relationships due to feeling undeserving of better treatment.

- Rationalizing abusive behavior as "normal" or "not that bad."

- Believing they need to "earn" love and acceptance.

8. Lack of Self-Identity

- Feeling lost or unsure about personal preferences, values, and goals.

- Adopting the interests or opinions of others to fit in.

- Struggling to recognize their own worth outside of the relationship.

If you're struggling with low self-esteem and people-pleasing, start by asking yourself—What would I do if I weren't afraid of disappointing someone? Your feelings, needs, and desires are just as valid as anyone else's. You don't have to earn your place in someone's life. You are enough—just as you are. And the right people will never ask you to prove it.

"Every new person you meet reveals a new aspect of yourself—if you pay close attention. This is something I come across often in deep discussions while helping and coaching people. A majority of those with low self-worth find themselves trapped in abusive relationships. The key lies in knowing your worth, looking within, and understanding your patterns. Identifying your "whys" and working on them changes everything.

*Now, there are two types of people in terms of dealing with low self-worth and fragile self esteem. Some seal it with **ego** and **arrogance**, turning bitter. These individuals make up the majority of humans walking this earth, narrating their sad stories about how someone mistreated or hurt them, holding onto that pain without growth. They in turn hurt the people who didn't hurt them reacting from their past wounds subconsciously.*

Then there are those rare souls who choose to look within. They **transform** *their hurt and trauma into invaluable* **wisdom**. *These people become more kind, more compassionate, and gain a clearer sense of* **reality**. *They don't allow their pain to define them but instead use it to evolve into their highest selves.* **"**

Imposter Syndrome in Narcissistic Abuse

Have you ever accomplished something and immediately thought, "I just got lucky" or "Someone's going to find out I don't deserve this"? No matter how hard you worked, there's a voice in your head whispering that you're not really good enough—that you're a fraud, and sooner or later, people will see the truth. That's imposter syndrome. And after narcissistic abuse, it feels even stronger.

Narcissistic abuse conditions you to doubt yourself. Every time you had an achievement, the narcissist either dismissed it, took credit for it, or made you feel like you still weren't enough. They convinced you that your success wasn't yours—it was a fluke, a mistake, or something you didn't really earn. Over time, you internalized their voice, and now, even when they're gone, their words still echo in your mind.

Think of it like carrying a funhouse mirror in your brain. No matter what you do, the reflection is distorted—you see failure where others see talent. Even when people praise you, your first instinct is to downplay it. If something goes wrong, you take all the blame. If something goes right, you assume it was an accident.

This is why, even after leaving the narcissist, you struggle to own your accomplishments. Their voice became part of your inner dialogue, making you feel like you're still not enough—no matter how much you achieve. But here's the truth: **You are not an imposter**. You didn't just "get lucky." You earned every step forward, despite the abuse, despite the doubt, despite the obstacles placed in your way.

Imposter syndrome is a deep-seated feeling of **inadequacy and self-doubt**, where survivors believe they are not as competent or deserving as others perceive them to be. Narcissistic abuse amplifies this by constantly **invalidating** the survivor's accomplishments, intelligence, and worth. Below are key signs:

1. **Feeling Like a Fraud**

   - Believing success is due to luck rather than skill.
   - Feeling undeserving of achievements, despite hard work.
   - Fear of being "exposed" as incompetent or fake.

2. **Perfectionism & Self-Criticism**

   - Setting **unrealistically high standards** and feeling like a failure if they aren't met.
   - Constantly focusing on flaws rather than strengths.
   - Feeling like nothing they do is "good enough."

3. **Fear of Judgment & Rejection**

   - Avoiding leadership roles or opportunities due to fear of failure.
   - Hesitating to speak up or share ideas, fearing they will be dismissed.
   - Constantly seeking validation to feel worthy.

4. **Difficulty Accepting Praise**

   - Brushing off compliments by attributing success to **external factors** (e.g. luck, help from others).
   - Feeling uncomfortable or suspicious when others acknowledge their abilities.
   - Doubting whether they truly deserve positive recognition.

5. **Overworking to Prove Worth**

    o   Taking on **excessive workloads** to validate self-worth.

    o   Feeling like they must work harder than others to be "good enough."

    o   Experiencing **burnout** due to constant self-imposed pressure.

6. **Comparing Oneself to Others**

    o   Believing others are naturally more talented, intelligent, or deserving.

    o   Feeling like they don't measure up, despite evidence of competence.

    o   Minimizing personal achievements while **amplifying others' successes.**

7. **Emotional Paralysis & Avoidance**

    o   Procrastinating or avoiding tasks due to fear of not doing them "perfectly."

    o   Feeling too overwhelmed to take risks or try new things.

    o   Holding back from **pursuing personal growth** due to fear of failure.

If you struggle with imposter syndrome, start asking yourself: What would I say to a friend who felt this way? You'd remind them of their hard work, their resilience, and their talent. Now, it's time to say those things to yourself. Because you are more than what the narcissist made you believe; you always have been.

Dissociation

Dissociation is a psychological response that causes a person to detach from their thoughts, emotions, memories, or sense of identity. After a traumatic event, individuals may experience some form of dissociation, either during the event or in the hours, days, or weeks that follow. For instance, the event may feel "unreal," or the person may feel disconnected, as though observing the situation from a distance, like watching it from outside their own body. In most cases, this dissociation tends to resolve on its own without the need for professional intervention.

Dissociation After Narcissistic Abuse

Have you ever felt like you're watching your own life from the outside, like a movie you're barely part of? Maybe you find yourself zoning out for long periods, struggling to remember conversations, or feeling emotionally numb—even when you should be feeling something. It's like your body is here, but you aren't. That's dissociation. And after narcissistic abuse, it can feel like the only way to survive.

Dissociation happens when your mind shuts down to protect you. When you were trapped in a toxic environment; constantly gaslit, manipulated, and made to feel unsafe—your brain learned that the best way to cope was to "check out." Instead of fighting or running, you froze. You learned to disconnect from the pain because feeling it in full force would have been unbearable.

Think of it like a circuit breaker shutting off power to prevent an overload. When the abuse was happening, your brain flipped the switch to keep you from breaking. And even now, when you're no longer in that situation, your mind still uses dissociation as a defense mechanism- because it doesn't realize the danger is over.

This is why you might feel emotionally detached, struggle to concentrate, or even forget big chunks of your past. Your brain is still protecting you the only way it knows how. But here's the truth: You are safe now. And you deserve to feel fully alive again.

Symptoms and signs of dissociative disorders vary based on their type and severity but may include:

- A sense of disconnection from oneself

- Difficulty managing intense emotions

- Sudden, unexplained mood shifts, such as feeling very sad without cause

- Depression, anxiety, or both

- A feeling that the world around you is distorted or unreal (known as 'derealization')

- Memory issues not linked to physical injury or medical conditions

- Other cognitive difficulties, such as trouble concentrating

- Significant lapses in memory, like forgetting key personal information

- Feeling driven to act in certain ways

- Identity confusion, such as behaving in ways that would typically be out of character or unacceptable for you.

If you struggle with dissociation, start by grounding yourself. Notice your surroundings. Feel your breath. Remind yourself that you are here, in this moment, and that you are no longer trapped in that cycle of abuse. Healing from dissociation isn't about forcing yourself to "snap out of it"—it's about slowly teaching your brain that it no longer needs to shut down to keep you safe.

Autoimmune Disease And Narcissistic Abuse

If you've endured narcissistic abuse, you've likely experienced not only emotional and psychological harm but also physical symptoms that seem to appear out of nowhere. One of the most alarming effects of long-term narcissistic abuse is the toll it can take on your body, sometimes contributing to the development of autoimmune diseases.

When your body is stuck in this heightened state for extended periods, your stress hormones, like cortisol, go haywire. Over time, this disrupts your immune system, making it more prone to inflammation and, in some cases, triggering autoimmune responses. Conditions like lupus, rheumatoid arthritis, fibromyalgia, and Hashimoto's thyroiditis have been linked to prolonged emotional stress.

But it's not just the stress—it's the silencing of your emotions. Think about it: How many times did you have to suppress your feelings just to survive? Anger, sadness, betrayal—they all stay trapped in your body when there's no safe outlet to release them. This emotional suppression can create a mind-body disconnect, leaving you vulnerable to physical ailments.

Additionally, narcissistic abuse often isolates you from supportive relationships, depriving you of the emotional connections needed to buffer against stress. Loneliness and lack of validation amplify the body's stress response, compounding the physical damage over time.

If you're struggling with an autoimmune disease after narcissistic abuse, it's not "all in your head," and you didn't imagine it. Your body has carried the burden of the abuse.

Trauma Bond

You might have heard the term trauma bond in reference to the abusive relationships. What is It? Trauma Bond is a complex emotional tie that develops between a survivor and their abuser, fueled by cycles of harm and occasional affection. Narcissistic abuse exploits this dynamic, creating extreme emotional swings that ensnare victims in a deep psychological connection, making escape extremely challenging. This bond is not built on love but rather on a psychological trap, one that keeps the victim tethered to their abuser despite the pain they endure. The very nature of narcissistic abuse, with its extreme highs and devastating lows, conditions the survivor to seek validation from the same person who is causing them harm.

The cycle typically begins with idealization, where the narcissist showers their victim with attention, affection, and admiration. This phase creates an intense emotional high, making the victim feel special, valued, and deeply connected to the narcissist. It is during this stage that the survivor unconsciously develops emotional dependency, believing they have found something rare and irreplaceable. However, this illusion is short-lived.

Victims often internalize the belief that they must work harder to "fix" the relationship, or somehow win back the love they once received. This confusion strengthens the trauma bond, a psychological attachment formed through cycles of intermittent reinforcement, where the narcissist offers moments of affection amid cruelty or neglect.

When the love bombing phase ends, the narcissist begins to devalue and manipulate you. They withdraw affection, criticize, or gaslight you, leaving you confused and desperate to return to the blissful early days of the relationship. This cycle of highs and lows creates cognitive dissonance—a mental struggle between the person you think they are (from the love bombing phase) and the person they reveal themselves to be.

Breaking free from a trauma bond requires more than just physical separation—it demands a rewiring of the survivor's mind. The addiction to the narcissist's approval must be replaced with self-awareness and self-validation. Understanding the psychological mechanisms at play is crucial in reclaiming one's autonomy. Healing begins when the survivor recognizes that the love they are chasing does not truly exist, and that the cycle will never change. The moment they stop seeking closure from the narcissist and start seeking it within themselves, they take the first step toward breaking free from the emotional chains that have kept them bounded.

CHAPTER 10

CHILDHOOD TRAUMA

"Anything that's wrong with you began as a survival mechanism in childhood."

The experiences we go through in our first ten years shape every decade that follows. During this critical period of rapid growth and development, our bodies, brains, and personalities are deeply influenced by our early environment. This is why childhood trauma can leave a lasting imprint on our mental, emotional, and physical well-being throughout life.

Childhood trauma takes many forms—physical or sexual abuse, neglect, or witnessing violence at home. But it's not always obvious. Relational trauma, such as a broken bond with a parent or caregiver, can be just as damaging. Trauma can also stem from external experiences, such as extreme bullying or large-scale events like a pandemic.

It isn't just about the pain endured— it's about the wounds that were never given the chance to heal. It's the silent suffering of a child who felt invisible, unloved, or unworthy. It's the emotional scars left by a toxic household, a narcissistic parent, or an environment where love was conditional. Trauma isn't just about what happened—it's also about what was missing protection, warmth, validation, and safety.

Childhood trauma can have a number of different signs in adults. For some people, it manifests as mental health disorders like anxiety or depression and autoimmune diseases in adulthood. Others may have trouble with relationships or struggle with addiction. And many people who have experienced traumatic events will have flashbacks or nightmares.

"Trauma can emotionally freeze us at the age it occurred."

1. **Difficulty in Trusting Others**

   If a child grows up in an environment where love was unpredictable, where the people who were supposed to provide safety were the ones causing harm, they learn one thing—trust is dangerous. As adults, they struggle to open up, fearing betrayal, rejection, or abandonment. They either build walls so high that no one can reach them or desperately cling to toxic relationships, afraid of being alone.

2. **Repeating Unhealthy Relationship Patterns**

   A child who witnesses emotional neglect, manipulation, or abuse unconsciously normalizes it. In adulthood, they often gravitate toward similar dynamics **believing that love and pain coexist.** Without even realizing it, they may end up in relationships where they are mistreated, simply because dysfunction feels familiar.

3. **Struggles with Self-Worth**

   When a child is constantly criticized, ignored, or made to feel like a burden, they internalize the belief that they are not enough. This carries into adulthood as deep-seated insecurities, self-doubt, and the inability to set boundaries. They overcompensate by overworking, over giving, or seeking validation—just to prove their worth.

4. **Anxiety, Depression, and Emotional Dysregulation**

   A childhood filled with fear and unpredictability wires the brain to stay in survival mode. As adults, they may experience chronic anxiety, panic attacks, depression, or even dissociation. Their nervous system is always on high alert, waiting for the next threat, even when there is none.

5. **Fear of Abandonment and Emotional Dependency**

   If a child was neglected or made to feel invisible, they grow up fearing abandonment. This manifests as an intense fear of rejection in relationships, leading to people-pleasing behaviours or tolerating mistreatment just to avoid being alone. The need for external validation becomes a survival mechanism.

6. **Hyper Independence**

As a childhood trauma response often develops as a survival mechanism in response to unmet emotional needs, neglect, or inconsistent caregiving. When a child repeatedly experiences situations where they cannot rely on others for support, validation, or safety, they may learn to depend solely on themselves. This can manifest in adulthood as an extreme reluctance to seek help, difficulty trusting others, and an overwhelming need to maintain control in all aspects of life. While self-sufficiency can be a strength, hyper independence can also lead to emotional isolation, burnout, and difficulty forming healthy, interdependent relationships.

"The clearest sign of childhood trauma is the desperate need to earn love from someone who withholds it, often a difficult or emotionally unavailable parent. In adulthood, this pattern repeats in romantic relationships, where the wounded inner child seeks validation from a toxic partner, believing that if they can just be "good enough," they will finally be loved. This cycle leads to self-sabotage—constantly bending, shrinking, and sacrificing oneself just to gain the affection that was never freely given."

The Mother Wound & Father Wound

Our first experiences with love, safety, and self-worth come from our parents. When those relationships are wounded; when a mother or father is absent, neglectful, critical, or emotionally unavailable—the effects don't end in childhood. They seep into adulthood, shaping how we see ourselves and how we navigate love.

The Mother Wound *(Lack of Nurturing & Emotional Safety)*

The mother is typically the first source of emotional connection. When this bond is damaged; through neglect, criticism, conditional love, or emotional unavailability—it creates a deep void.

In adulthood, the mother wound often manifests as:

- **Struggles with self-worth** – Feeling never "good enough" and seeking external validation.

- **People-pleasing tendencies** – Overextending in relationships to earn love and approval.

- **Difficulty receiving love and care** – Feeling uncomfortable with affection or sabotaging relationships where love is freely given.

- **Fear of rejection and abandonment** – A deep-seated anxiety that being authentic will drive people away.

- **Attracting emotionally unavailable partners** – Seeking out those who mirror the neglect or emotional coldness of the mother.

Women with a mother wound often struggle with self-nurturing, feeling guilty for prioritizing their own needs. Men with a mother wound may seek partners to "mother" them or have trouble forming deep emotional connections.

The Father Wound *(Lack of Protection & Validation)*

A father provides security, guidance, and validation. When a father is absent, dismissive, abusive or emotionally distant, it leaves deep scars.

In adulthood, the father wound often manifests as:

- **Fear of abandonment** – Seeking security in relationships, often tolerating mistreatment out of fear of being alone.

- **Attracting controlling or emotionally unavailable partners** – Repeating the pattern of chasing after validation.

- **Struggles with self-confidence** – Feeling unworthy, unseen, or incapable.

- **Overachieving or perfectionism** – Trying to prove worth through success or external accomplishments.

- **Fear of intimacy** – Associating closeness with pain or rejection, leading to emotional walls in relationships.

For women, a father wound can lead to seeking validation from emotionally distant men, mistaking neglect for love. For men, it may create identity struggles, difficulty expressing emotions, or a tendency to shut down in relationships.

"A child first enemy is an unhealed parent"

Breaking the Cycle

Breaking the cycle of the mother and father wound begins with deep self-awareness. It requires unlearning the belief that love must be earned through suffering. The child within you still longs for the nurturing, validation, and safety that was absent, but as an adult, you now have the power to give yourself what was once denied.

Healing is painful because it forces you to confront the voids left behind—the moments you needed comfort but received coldness, the times you sought approval but were met with criticism. It demands that you stop chasing love in places it was never meant to be found. Instead of seeking a partner to fix the wounds of your past, healing asks you to become the parent you always needed.

It is a process of learning to trust yourself after years of being told you were unworthy. It is choosing relationships that feel safe, not familiar. It is walking away from cycles of neglect, even when they feel like home. Healing does not mean the pain disappears overnight, but it does mean that your past no longer dictates your future. You are not broken. You are not unlovable. The love you spent your entire life searching for has always been within you, waiting to be reclaimed.

CHAPTER 11

THE WEIGHT OF WOMANHOOD AND THE SILENT SACRIFICES

Society has long romanticized a woman's ability to tolerate pain, mistaking endurance for strength. But true strength is not in suffering silently—it is in recognizing one's worth and refusing to be confined by abuse. For women caught in narcissistic relationships, especially mothers, life turns into a relentless battle for survival, shielding their children from harm, overcompensating for the narcissist's neglect, and carrying the weight of emotional and financial burdens alone.

The Burden of Overcompensation: A Single Mother's Struggle After Narcissistic Abuse

Being with a narcissistic partner does not mean co-parenting, it means **single** parenting and **counter** parenting within a relationship. Narcissists do not participate in household responsibilities, nor do they contribute meaningfully to a child's upbringing, whether in academics, emotional support, or daily care. Instead, they create more obstacles, leaving the entire weight of parenting on your shoulders while simultaneously criticizing you for how you handle it. You are constantly gaslit into believing you are the problem, that you are failing, while they remain absent—either physically or emotionally.

"*Women in narcissistic abuse become very lonely. I believe people truly do not know the meaning of loneliness unless they are in the narcissistic relationship and experiencing it first hand. It takes a lot of strength and courage to stand up for yourself and your child without any kind of a support to pull yourself from the darkness and face the unkind world. Women become silent and numb in narcissistic relationship because they have endured so much that nothing shocks them anymore. **Every fear they once had, has already come true and they have reached the point where they cannot imagine anything worse.**"*

The financial burden of single parenting is heavy, but **it becomes suffocating when you finally decide to leave**. Separation from a narcissist is never just about physical distance—it's about untangling yourself from their web of control, and finances are one of their strongest weapons. The moment you choose to walk away, the reality of financial abuse becomes undeniable. In my case, my ex-husband had already used money as a tool of manipulation while we were together—ensuring I remained dependent, making unilateral financial decisions, and even sabotaging our child's education. When I left, he escalated the abuse—legal threats, withdrawal of financial support, and false accusations designed to drain my resources and keep me trapped in a battle I never wanted to fight.

The burden of overcompensation takes a toll, forcing single mothers to pour from an already empty cup, constantly trying to fill the void left by the narcissist's neglect. Yet, many women remain in these abusive marriages, held back by fear, financial dependence, societal pressure, or the desperate hope that things will change.

Divorcing a narcissist is even worse. They will use every legal loophole, every ounce of manipulation, to **prolong the process, exhaust you financially, and make you regret ever leaving**. They will delay proceedings, refuse to cooperate, and, in many cases, attempt to financially cripple you so that returning to them seems like the only option. This is not just about the legal system—this is about **power and control**; about making sure you never truly escape their grasp.

And then comes the emotional exhaustion—the kind that no one prepares you for. **The guilt. The overcompensation. The constant crushing fear of not being enough.** Single mothers who escape narcissistic abuse often go to extreme lengths to ensure their child never feels the absence of the father. You try to fill the emotional void, provide endless reassurance, and shield them from any pain or struggle. You overextend yourself financially, emotionally, and physically trying to play both roles, trying to be everything at once.

But the truth is, **overcompensation comes at a cost.** It drains you in ways you don't even realize—mentally, emotionally, financially, and physically. You pour so much into making sure your child never feels the void that you end up neglecting your own needs. **The exhaustion becomes a silent companion, and the weight of doing it all alone starts to feel unbearable.**

In my book, I want to address this brutal reality—the **silent suffering of single mothers** after narcissistic abuse. The exhaustion of parenting alone, the financial strain of separation, the guilt of trying to overcompensate, and the battle of constantly proving to yourself that you are enough. But most importantly, I want survivors to understand this:

You are already enough!! Your child does not need an overworked, depleted mother trying to fill an impossible void. They need a present, safe parent, emotionally stable and available mother who chooses peace over perfection, toxic marriage over safety. The absence of a toxic father is not a gap to be filled; it is a wound that will heal over time, as long as you are there to guide them with love and truth. **You do not have to be everything. You just have to be you.**

When a mother stays in a toxic marriage, she's weak. When she leaves she's selfish. There is no winning and you will be judged either ways. So do what's best for your children. No one will protect them like you do!!

Societal Conditioning And Self-Sacrifice Glorified

From the time we are little girls, we are conditioned to believe that our worth is measured by how much we endure. We are praised for being selfless, for sacrificing our needs, for putting others first. A woman who gives endlessly—whether in marriage, motherhood, or society—is seen as "good." But the moment she prioritizes herself, even in the smallest ways, she is met with judgment. This conditioning is even more brutal for single mothers. Society places an unbearable weight on their shoulders, expecting them to be both parents, financial providers, caretakers, and emotional shock absorbers—all while making sure they never complain or collapse under the pressure.

A single mother who dares to take time for herself is often criticized. If she steps out, dresses up or enjoys a moment away from responsibilities, she is labeled selfish, irresponsible or even characterless. But if she suffers silently, neglecting herself, working herself to exhaustion, tolerating abuse and staying in toxic environments "for the sake of her children," she is celebrated as a strong woman. **Tolerating mistreatment is seen as a virtue, while standing up against it is condemned as rebellion.** The moment a woman asserts herself, refuses to be exploited, or sets firm boundaries, she is instantly labeled as "too much." She is called selfish, difficult, or even immoral. Character assassination begins the moment she decides she will no longer be society's doormat.

It is time to break this cycle. Self-care is not selfish—it is survival. A mother who nurtures herself, who reclaims her time and joy, is setting an example for her children. She is teaching them that a woman's life is valuable beyond her service to others. Children do not thrive watching their mother be a martyr—they thrive when they see her as a whole, fulfilled person. Breaking free from this conditioning means rejecting guilt, setting boundaries, and embracing the truth that you deserve rest, pleasure, and freedom—just as much as anyone else. The world will always try to shame a woman who refuses to be broken, but the moment she chooses herself, she is already free.

Why Do Women Stay In Abusive Marriages?

Leaving an abusive marriage is not as simple as people think. The most common question survivors hear is, **"Why didn't you just leave?"** But the reality is that abuse is never just physical—it is psychological, financial, and emotional. It is a slow and deliberate process that conditions the victim to feel trapped, helpless and incapable of escape. Women do not stay because they enjoy the abuse—they stay because their abuser has systematically destroyed their ability to leave. Here's why:

1. **Financial Dependency – The Abuser's Most Strategic Weapon**
   Financial abuse is one of the most effective tools an abuser uses to keep a woman trapped. This is not accidental—it is a **carefully crafted strategy** to strip the victim of independence and options. Narcissistic abusers often ensure that their partners are either:

   o   Not working (convincing them to quit their job or never pursue a career).

   o   Financially dependent, even if they are earning (controlling their income, restricting access to bank accounts, or keeping all assets in their name).

   o   Constantly dealing with financial sabotage (sudden job loss due to the abuser's interference, forcing them to take on debt, or ruining their credit).

In my own experience, financial control was used as a weapon long before I even realized I was being abused. My ex made unilateral financial decisions, kept me unaware of crucial financial matters, and ensured I had limited resources. The moment I decided to leave, financial abuse escalated—withdrawal of support, legal battles, and attempts to cripple me financially so that I would feel I had no choice but to return. This is why many women stay: **because survival outside of the marriage seems financially impossible.**

2. **Trauma Bond – The Psychological Handcuffs**
   Trauma bonding is one of the most **invisible but powerful chains** that keep women stuck in abusive marriages. Unlike what people assume, abusers

are not always cruel—they are calculated. They create cycles of abuse and affection—extreme cruelty followed by love-bombing, apologies, and short periods of peace. This unpredictable cycle conditions the victim to seek **validation from the very person causing them pain.**

Women in trauma bonds often:

o   Believe the abuser will change.

o   Blame themselves for the abuse ("Maybe if I do things differently, he will stop hurting me").

o   Feel addicted to the intermittent affection from the abuser.

o   Experience extreme confusion and emotional dependence on the abuser's approval.

Narcissists are particularly skilled at using trauma bonding because they manipulate their victims into **believing that leaving means losing love.** This is why even when the abuse is unbearable, the victim often stays— **because the abuser has convinced them that no one else will ever love them.**

3.   **Societal Taboo & Manipulation by Family and Society**
     In many cultures, leaving a marriage; especially as a woman is considered shameful. Society, rather than protecting the victim, often:

o   **Blames the woman** for the failure of the marriage.

o   Encourages her to "adjust" or "compromise" for the sake of family honor.

o   Invalidates her pain by saying, "All marriages have problems."

o   Forces her to stay for the sake of the children, ignoring the psychological damage of an abusive household.

Family manipulation is another major factor. Women are often pressured by their own parents or relatives to **"keep the family together"**, sometimes even being forced to return to an abusive husband because divorce is seen as a disgrace. Narcissists take full advantage of this societal mindset—they **paint the victim as difficult, unstable, or even crazy** to ensure that no one supports her when she finally tries to leave.

4. **Fear of Retaliation – The Unspoken Threat**
Leaving an abuser is not just difficult; it can be dangerous. Many women stay because they fear retaliation:

   o   Threats of violence

   o   Legal battles over child custody

   o   Ruined reputation due to smear campaigns

   o   Harassment and stalking after leaving

Narcissistic abusers do not simply "let go." They escalate the abuse if they feel they are losing control. This fear of **what will happen if they leave,** keeps many victims trapped longer than they want to be.

5. **Shame – The Silent Prison**
Shame is one of the strongest emotional barriers preventing women from leaving an abusive marriage. Society conditions women to believe that a failed marriage is **their** failure, no matter the circumstances. The shame of being labeled a "divorcee," a "broken woman," or a "bad wife" can feel unbearable.

Women in narcissistic marriages also feel shame because:

   o   They are embarrassed that they "chose" the wrong partner.

   o   They fear being judged for tolerating the abuse for so long.

   o   They worry about how others will perceive them, especially if the narcissist has manipulated their social circle.

Shame isolates victims. It keeps them silent. It convinces them that **staying and suffering quietly is better than leaving and being judged.**

6. **Children – The Most Manipulated Factor**

A mother's love for her children is **exploited by the abuser** to keep her in the marriage. Women often stay because they believe:

- A broken home will harm the children more than staying.
- The abuser will turn the children against them.
- They will lose custody in a legal battle.
- They will struggle to financially provide for the children alone.

Narcissists use children as **weapons**—threatening to take them away, poisoning their minds against the mother and using them as leverage to maintain control. Many women stay because they fear the legal system will fail them, leaving their children vulnerable to the abuser.

But what is often overlooked is this: **staying in an abusive home damages children far more than leaving ever will.** A child who grows up witnessing abuse will either normalize it or repeat the cycle in their own relationships. **Leaving is not just about saving yourself—it's about saving your children too.**

The truth is, **women in abusive marriages do not stay because they want to. They stay because leaving has been made nearly impossible.** Financial dependency, psychological trauma, societal manipulation, lack of support, shame, fear for their children, and the threat of retaliation all create a prison that many cannot escape easily.

This is why my book will address **not just why women stay, but how they can leave; strategically and safely.** Understanding the mind of a narcissist, recognizing financial and emotional abuse, and building a plan for escape is essential. Most importantly, women need to know: **the abuse is not their fault, and they are not alone.**

> *Victims are trained to get abused in the society; specially women. Victims of abuse survivors get away only to be abused by someone else. Predators are adept at finding their prey. They pick up on cues nobody*

else can see—psychological, behavioral or non verbal and none of it is under victims control and none of it is victims fault.

"Leaving is hard. But staying is soul-shattering. And no one deserves to live in a prison built by someone else's cruelty."

When You Feel Left Behind

Narcissistic relationships have a way of making you feel like you're stuck in quicksand while the rest of the world runs marathons. Financially, career-wise, and even emotionally, it can feel like everyone is lightyears ahead, building their dreams while you're just trying to survive.

The truth is, narcissistic abuse drains not only your resources but your spirit. It leaves you constantly firefighting; keeping your head above water while trying to shield your child from the storm. Surviving becomes the priority.

Never forget: **protecting your child and keeping yourself safe was your greatest accomplishment.** It's hard to see it this way when society measures success through wealth and accolades. But surviving narcissistic abuse is a monumental achievement that often goes unseen and uncelebrated.

Yes, others may seem ahead in life, but no one has walked your path. No one knows the strength it takes to come out the other side.

"I met a little elf-man, once,
Down where the lilies blow.
I asked him why he was so small,
And why he didn't grow.
He slightly frowned, and with his eye
He looked me through and through.
'I'm just as big for me,' said he,
'As you are big for you.'"
– John Kendrick Bangs

You are as big as you need to be. Your journey is uniquely yours, and it's one of courage. Don't let the illusion of comparison steal the joy of what you've achieved—**freedom**. You've saved yourself and your child, and that is more than enough.

Why Narcissistic Men Target Kind Women

Narcissistic men are drawn to kind and empathetic women because they see them as ideal targets for their manipulation and control. Here's why narcissistic men often prey on kind women:

1. **Empathy**: Kind women are naturally empathetic and deeply attuned to the emotions of others. They are willing to listen, comfort, and validate, which narcissistic men exploit to gain attention and emotional support.

2. **Conflict Avoidance**: Kind women prefer to avoid conflict and maintain peace in relationships. This makes them less likely to challenge or call out the narcissist's toxic behavior, allowing the abuse to continue unchecked.

3. **Forgiving Nature**: Narcissistic men thrive on the forgiving nature of kind women. They know that Kind women are more likely to give them the benefit of the doubt, even when the narcissist's behavior is harmful.

4. **Selflessness**: Kind women often prioritize others' needs over their own, making them easy to exploit. A narcissistic man will take advantage of this trait to ensure his desires and demands come first, leaving the woman drained and unfulfilled.

5. **Desire to Please**: Many kind women feel a deep need to make others happy. Narcissistic men manipulate this desire, ensuring that the woman bends over backward to meet their impossible standards while ignoring her own well-being.

6. **Belief in Redemption**: Kind women tend to believe in people's capacity for change and often hold on to the hope that their partner will improve.

Narcissistic men exploit this optimism, cycling between moments of charm and cruelty to keep the woman emotionally invested in the relationship.

7. **Reluctance to Judge**: A kind woman's reluctance to see the narcissist as "bad" or "toxic" gives him the opportunity to manipulate her further. She may try to justify his behavior by blaming it on his past, stress, or external circumstances, instead of recognizing his deliberate choices.

8. **Guilt Sensitivity**: Narcissistic men are skilled at using guilt as a weapon. They know that kind women, who are sensitive and empathetic, will feel responsible for the narcissist's unhappiness or problems, making it easier for them to control her.

9. **Encouragement and Validation**: Kind women are naturally supportive and nurturing. They encourage their partner's growth and provide unwavering validation, which feeds the narcissist's insatiable ego. He will take the praise without reciprocating, leaving her emotionally depleted.

10. **Emotional Resilience**: Narcissists know that kind women are often resilient and capable of enduring emotional pain. This resilience allows the narcissist to prolong the abuse, knowing the woman will continue to try and "make it work" despite the suffering.

11. **Loyalty**: Kind women are incredibly loyal, even to their own detriment. Narcissistic men exploit this loyalty to trap them in the relationship, using promises of change or fleeting moments of affection to keep them tethered.

12. **Vulnerability to Manipulation**: Narcissistic men excel at identifying the vulnerabilities of kind women, such as their fear of abandonment or rejection. They use these fears to manipulate and maintain control, creating a dynamic where the woman feels she must constantly prove her worth.

13. **Subtle Conditioning**: Narcissistic men condition kind women to believe that they are the problem in the relationship. They gaslight them into

thinking their needs or boundaries are unreasonable, eroding their self-esteem and making them more submissive.

14. **Ideal Targets for Love Bombing**: Kind women are more susceptible to the narcissist's initial charm during the love-bombing phase. The narcissist uses exaggerated affection, flattery, and promises of a perfect future to win her over, knowing her kind heart will respond with trust and devotion.

In summary, narcissistic men target kind women because their empathy, forgiveness, and selflessness make them more likely to tolerate manipulation and abuse. These women's strengths are twisted into weaknesses in the hands of a narcissist. It's vital for kind women to recognize these patterns, set firm boundaries, and prioritize their own well-being to protect themselves from such toxic relationships.

Emotional health of a victim

By now, your emotional health has been shattered. If you have children, they rely entirely on you for their emotional well-being; yet the very person responsible for their existence has strategically destroyed yours. There should be a special place in hell for those who strategically break a mother's spirit, shouldn't there?

No one truly understands what you're going through; the relentless struggles of a narcissistic relationship, from the smallest manipulations to the most overwhelming betrayals. To the outside world, everything appears normal, yet behind closed doors, he has been creating endless hurdles, making even the most basic human needs—food, shelter, and security, nearly impossible for you to access.

He weaponizes your child against you, leaving you trapped in an agonizing dilemma: Should you cave in, surrender to his demands, and become his puppet just to ensure your child's education? But then reality strikes; staying means exposing your child to the same abuse, subtle yet deeply damaging.

A child cannot comprehend narcissistic manipulation, but they suffer its consequences. The toxic environment he has created is no place for a child to grow. Living with one loving parent is far healthier than being stuck in a dysfunctional household where abuse is normalized. Children raised in such chaos often grow up believing that love and abuse coexist, dooming them to repeat the same cycles in their own relationships. No mother wants that for her child.

So, you decide to leave. But he doesn't let you go easily. He turns the divorce into a battlefield, using your child as a pawn, exploiting the legal system that fails to recognize the insidious nature of narcissistic abuse. Financially, he has drained you; sabotaging your career, depleting your savings, ensuring you are never independent enough to escape. He has waged a smear campaign, turning your own family against you, leaving you without support, without a home, without options. I will never forget how he abandoned us, leaving me to struggle alone for food and shelter in a foreign land.

And then, the shame creeps in. You start questioning everything; when did it all begin? Why did you marry him? Guilt consumes you: *How could you have chosen such a toxic father for your child?* And just like that, the cycle traps you once again.

Society only makes it worse. Divorce is still stigmatized, and instead of offering support, families invalidate your pain. They would rather see you suffer, trapped, broken or even dead in a toxic marriage than take a stand and help you break free. Financial independence is your only escape, yet they dismiss your struggles, failing to recognize abuse because they have no awareness of what it truly looks like. **Worst of all, it's often women themselves who perpetuate this ignorance, conditioned to accept abuse as "normal."**

This is the harsh reality of surviving narcissistic abuse in a society that refuses to see it. But recognizing it is the first step towards reclaiming your life, and you are not crazy—this is real and you deserve freedom. I know there is a lot of invalidation which will keep you In the state of confusion. But trust me what you are experiencing is real. You need to take a stand for you and for your child/ children. *The amount of strength it takes to be alone in stead of poorly surrounding yourself is extremely underrated. If you are one of them; Be Proud!*

> *How a person is treated in their moment of pain influences their next steps. When met with kindness, they learn to trust themselves. When met with cruelty, they feel shame; not because they deserve it, but because they were made to feel that way in a moment of vulnerability.*

Personally, I am deeply grateful for the people I met during the darkest phase of my life—the ones who offered even the smallest support, who validated my experience when I felt invisible. In my lowest moments, they extended a helping hand. When I couldn't think straight, they grounded me. When panic attacks consumed me, they held me. When I feared losing my child, they gave me the strength to keep fighting.

These seemingly small gestures meant everything to me. I will forever cherish the kindness they showed. This journey has been painfully isolating, but those who provided unwavering support are my true heroes.

> *"Sometimes there is no support system. Its just you, the universe and a vision only you can see"*

Will Narcissist ever change?

The answer is a resounding "No." A narcissist will never truly change. They are fundamentally deluded and lack the self-awareness necessary for transformation. Their entire worldview is built on a distorted sense of reality, where they believe their own lies and manipulate the perception of events to suit their needs and situational requirements. They are incapable of seeing reality for what it is because doing so would shatter the carefully constructed facade they've built to protect their fragile ego. Admitting fault or acknowledging harm is not just uncomfortable for them—it is unthinkable.

Narcissists live in a bubble of self-deception, twisting events, conversations, and relationships to fit their narrative. They do not see the truth—they only see what benefits them in the moment. For example, when confronted with evidence of their abusive behavior, they will deny, deflect, or reinterpret it in a way that absolves them of responsibility. They may even accuse the victim of being the abusive one, flipping the script to portray themselves as the misunderstood, injured party. This deluded sense of reality ensures they never have to face their flaws or take accountability.

This is why calling out a narcissist is extremely dangerous. The moment they sense that you've figured them out, they will go into overdrive to protect their image and power. They will see you as a threat that needs to be eliminated, not someone to reason with. A narcissist will stop at nothing to destroy anyone who exposes them. They will smear your reputation, manipulate others to turn against you, and escalate their abuse to punish you for daring to challenge their facade. For your safety, the best approach is to recognize their tactics quietly, gather your strength, and plan your escape without tipping them off. Engaging in direct confrontation will only provoke their wrath and leave you vulnerable to their retaliation.

In therapy, particularly in couples' counseling, this delusion becomes even more dangerous. Rather than using the space to address their issues, a narcissist will weaponize therapy to further harm the victim. They will throw their partner under the bus, portraying themselves as the true victim in the relationship. They will spin stories, exaggerate flaws, and manipulate the therapist into sympathizing with them. Unless the therapist is highly skilled in recognizing narcissistic patterns, the sessions often end up re-traumatizing the victim, as the narcissist twists the narrative to suit their needs. Therapy becomes just another stage for their manipulation, not a tool for growth.

The inability to change is rooted in the very essence of narcissism. Narcissists lack the capacity for genuine self-reflection because their ego is too fragile to withstand the truth. To admit wrongdoing or to acknowledge they are the problem would mean confronting their inadequacies, something they are psychologically unequipped to do. Their entire identity depends on maintaining their delusions of superiority, control, and righteousness. Any challenge to this delusion is met with rage, denial or further manipulation. Due to its deep psychological and neurological roots, narcissism is highly resistant to change. Unlike other behavioral patterns that can be unlearned, narcissistic traits form the foundation of the individual's identity.

For the victim, holding on to the hope that the narcissist will change is not only futile but dangerous. It keeps them trapped in the cycle of abuse, enduring the same patterns of harm in the belief that things will eventually improve. But the hard truth is that a narcissist will never wake up one day and realize the pain they've caused. They will never develop empathy or accountability. Instead, they will continue to adapt their tactics to maintain control, always prioritizing their needs above the well-being of others.

CHAPTER 12

BREAKING FREE

Leaving a narcissistic relationship, especially with a covert narcissist, requires careful planning and strategic execution. They are highly perceptive and closely monitor your actions, especially once discussions of separation or divorce arise. A well-thought-out exit plan is essential to ensure your and your child's safety and minimize manipulation or retaliation. Let's explore some practical steps to help you navigate this process effectively.

1. Detachment: The First Step Towards Emotional Freedom

Managing triggers from narcissistic abuse, especially when living under the same roof, can be incredibly challenging. Detachment is indeed the first stage. and here's a deeper look at how to approach it:

1. **Understanding Emotional Detachment:** Detachment doesn't mean emotionally disconnecting from your own feelings. It means recognizing and separating yourself from the narcissist's manipulations. It's about protecting your peace by refusing to engage in their games. Narcissists thrive on your emotional reactions, so the goal is to not give them that satisfaction.

2. **Recognize the Manipulation:** Narcissists will push your buttons to provoke reactions. Being aware of this can help you prepare. Whenever you feel triggered, take a step back and ask yourself, "Is this really about me, or is it part of their manipulation?"

3. **Reframing Your Mindset:** Reframing means changing the way you perceive the situation. Instead of seeing the narcissist's behavior as an

attack on you, view it as a reflection of their own insecurities and need for control. By reframing, you lessen the emotional impact their behavior has on you.

4. **Practice Neutral Responses:** When a narcissist tries to provoke you, practice giving neutral, non-committal responses. For example, if they accuse or criticize you, simply say "Okay" or "I understand" and move on. This leaves them without the fuel they need to continue their attack.

5. **Focus on Yourself:** Reconnect with your own feelings, needs, and desires. Engaging in activities that center on your well-being (journaling, meditation, exercise) can help you stay grounded and reduce the emotional impact of the narcissist's behavior.

6. **Set Boundaries:** If possible, set clear and firm boundaries. Narcissists will test limits, so it's essential to reinforce your boundaries consistently, even if they don't respect them at first.

7. **Keep a Journal:** Documenting your experiences can help you process your emotions and maintain perspective. Writing down your triggers and how you handled them can be a powerful tool for emotional clarity.

8. **Seek Support:** Even if you're detaching emotionally, it's still crucial to have a support system. Whether it's a therapist, support group, or trusted friend, talking things through with someone who understands can provide validation and help you stay grounded.

With practice, detachment becomes easier, and you'll regain control over your emotional responses, making it harder for the narcissist to provoke you.

> *"There's a beautiful verse in the Bhagavad Gita that says: Detachment is not that you own nothing, detachment is that nothing owns you"*

2. Seeking Help & Understanding Your Legal Rights

One of the most crucial steps in breaking free from a narcissist is seeking help from social services and educating yourself about your legal rights. However, this must be done with extreme caution. A narcissist will not only resist your attempts to seek support, but they will also go to great lengths to manipulate the system against you.

Why You Must Keep This Hidden from the Narcissist

The moment a narcissist senses that you are trying to escape their control, they shift into damage control mode. They will manipulate social services into believing they are the victim. Narcissists are skilled at playing the wounded party, twisting the narrative so that you appear unstable, abusive, or neglectful.

- File false reports against you accusing you of parental alienation, domestic abuse or even financial misconduct.

- Retaliate with intensified abuse, including physical, emotional and financial coercion, to punish you for taking action.

- Try to make you hostage, either physically by restricting your movement or psychologically by isolating you from support and making you financially dependent.

Gather Documentation- Collect evidence of abuse (texts, emails, recordings where legally permitted, financial records, medical reports, or testimonies). Keep these stored securely and outside the home where the narcissist cannot access them.

Consult a Lawyer in Secrecy- Find a lawyer specializing in domestic abuse, custody issues, and financial exploitation. Do not use shared devices to research legal help. Consider using incognito mode, a friend's phone or a public library computer.

Reach Out to Social Services Quietly- If you need assistance with housing, financial aid or restraining orders, contact social services only when it is safe to do so. Some organizations offer discreet exit strategies to help survivors leave abusive situations without tipping off their abuser.

Secure an Escape Plan- If the narcissist shows signs of extreme retaliation (threatening your safety, finances, or children), create a safety plan. This could involve arranging a safe place to stay in advance. Keeping important documents and emergency funds hidden or with a trusted person. Informing only people you deeply trust about your plan.

Never Confront the Narcissist About Legal Action- The moment they realize you are taking steps to break free, they will escalate their tactics. They will lie, smear your reputation, manipulate your children or even use the legal system as a tool to drain you emotionally and financially.

3. Financial Independence & Rebuilding Stability

Narcissists use financial abuse as a tool of control—limiting your access to money, sabotaging your career or making you financially dependent so that leaving becomes nearly impossible. Breaking free requires regaining financial independence:

- Open a private bank account (if you don't have one) and secure your financial documents.
- Save emergency funds quietly, even if it means small amounts at a time.
- Separate finances legally if applicable (joint accounts, loans, or assets).
- Seek employment or remote work opportunities to establish an independent income stream.
- Change passwords on financial accounts to prevent unauthorized access.

Why this matters: Financial security gives you the ability to exit safely and prevents the narcissist from using money and keeping track of expenses.

4. Execute Your Plan

Choose the Right Time— Timing is crucial when leaving a narcissistic relationship. Plan your exit when your partner is least likely to be around or paying attention—this could be when they are at work, engaged in a personal hobby, out with friends or preoccupied with something that keeps them distracted. The goal is to minimize confrontation and avoid an immediate reaction that could escalate into manipulation, guilt-tripping or even aggression.

Ensure a Safe and Smooth Transition:

- **Have Your Essentials Ready:** Gather important documents (passports, IDs, birth certificates, financial records, legal papers), money, keys, medication, and any other necessities in advance. Keep them in a secure, **accessible place.**

- **Arrange for Support:** If possible, have a trusted friend, family member, or professional help you during the transition. A support system—even a single person can make a huge difference in keeping you grounded and safe.

- **Secure Housing and Finances:** If you haven't already, ensure you have a place to stay and a way to support yourself, even temporarily. Consider shelters, short-term rentals, or staying with someone you trust until you can establish stability.

- **Avoid Direct Confrontation:** Do not disclose your plans to the narcissist ahead of time. Many will use manipulation, gaslighting, love bombing, or threats to make you stay. If you must communicate, do so from a safe distance or through a legal intermediary.

Final Step: Leave Without Looking Back

Once you step away, focus on securing your well-being and maintaining *No Contact* (or strict boundaries if co-parenting). Expect emotional challenges but remind yourself that leaving was necessary for your freedom and healing. The hardest part is over; you have broken free. Now, it's time to reclaim your life.

5. No Contact

No contact is the most effective tool to stop this toxic cycle, allowing you to rebuild your sense of self. The decision to go no contact is met with immense resistance. ***The narcissist will not let you go easily***. They play on your emotions, using guilt, threats or charm to pull you back in. They may tell you that they've changed or that you're the one causing the problems. But understand this—closure from a narcissist is an illusion. They will never give you the validation or understanding you need because they are incapable of seeing you as a person with feelings, needs and boundaries. To them, you are just a tool for their supply and their primary goal is to keep you hooked in their game.

No contact is not just about cutting off communication, it's about protecting your mind, emotions, and soul from the ongoing manipulation. It's about creating the space you need to heal, to regain your clarity, and to rediscover who you truly are. At first, the withdrawal symptoms will feel overwhelming. The narcissist's voice may still echo in your head, and the urge to contact them may be strong. But every time you resist, you are taking back a piece of your power.

Any and all contact with the narcissist is an opportunity to abuse and retraumatize the target. They know what they are doing and their cruelty. You don't owe them truth because they will use and abuse and torture you. A big no to sharing your future plans. They have lied to you all your life. Be extremely careful what you share with them.

You'll begin to realize that every attempt to engage with them, even in anger or frustration, is just another form of supplying them with the emotional reaction they crave. Their manipulation thrives on your responses. The moment you stop engaging, you take away their control. You stop feeding the beast that thrives on your pain and confusion. The more information they get about you and your life the more they sabotage your happiness and create subtle hurdles for you.

Sever all communication:

Block their phone number, emails and social media. The path to liberation from a narcissist begins with resolutely severing all lines of communication. By blocking their phone number, emails and social media accounts, you dismantle the avenues through which they can continue to inflict harm.

- Block their phone number, emails, and social media.

- Do not respond to texts or calls, even if they seem harmless.

- Ignore voicemails, letters or other means of contact.

- If necessary, change your number and email address.

Recognize Their Manipulation Tactics:

The narcissist will not accept No Contact easily. Expect them to try different tactics to get you back into their control:

- Love-bombing: They suddenly act like the person you fell in love with.

- Guilt-tripping: "After everything we've been through, you're really ignoring me?"

- Smear campaigns: They will spread lies to damage your reputation.

- Fake emergencies: "I'm sick. I need you." (They are lying.)

- Using flying monkeys: Mutual friends or family may try to get you to respond.

- Hoovering: They will try anything to suck you back into the cycle.

Recognizing these tactics for what they are is crucial. They are not real; they are manipulation.

Reframing Your Mindset

The narcissist wants you to believe that

No Contact is cruel or unfair. In reality, it is your way of protecting yourself. You are not being mean, you are choosing yourself over abuse. Every time you doubt your decision, remind yourself of why you left.

Stick to Business-Only Contact if Necessary

If you share children, work together, or have legal matters to settle, full No Contact may not be possible. In such cases:

- Keep communication strictly business-like and minimal.

- Use email or a legal parenting app to document conversations.

- Do not respond to personal attacks—stay neutral and unemotional.

- If they escalate, involve legal authorities instead of engaging.

The narcissist will test your boundaries again and again. They will wait months, even years, for the perfect moment to try to pull you back in. **Stay strong. Stay no contact.** Every time you respond, you give them a way back into your life. Every time you ignore them, you take back your power.

No contact doesn't just help you get out of the relationship—it helps you get out of the *trauma* of the relationship. It's about reclaiming your space and your peace and it begins with not allowing them to continue taking pieces of you. Every day you stay no contact, you choose yourself over their manipulation. You protect your sanity, and you begin to heal.

CHAPTER 13

HEALING: A JOURNEY BACK TO YOURSELF

Healing is not about forgetting what happened—it's about reclaiming the parts of yourself that were lost along the way. It is an unlearning of survival mechanisms that no longer serve you and a relearning of self-trust, self-love, and inner peace. True healing isn't a destination but a continuous process of choosing yourself every day, even when the past tries to pull you back. It requires patience, self-compassion, and the courage to sit with your pain instead of running from it. Healing is in the moments when you recognize your triggers but no longer let them control you. It is in the boundaries you set, the self-worth you rebuild, and the freedom you give yourself to feel joy again. It is not about becoming someone new but returning to who you were always meant to be without fear, without shame, and without the weight of someone else's wounds dictating your life.

"You have to be willing to be vulnerable in order in order to grow. You can't heal what you hide. Healing teaches you to open your heart and crates boundaries. Healing is messy but its transformative."

The Healing Process After Narcissistic Abuse

Healing begins with recognizing that what you went through was real and damaging. Narcissistic abuse distorts your perception of reality, making you question your own experiences and feelings. Give yourself permission to acknowledge the pain without minimizing it.

Healing from narcissistic abuse is a journey of reclaiming your identity, rebuilding your self-worth, and learning to trust yourself again. It requires breaking free from the psychological chains of manipulation, gaslighting, and self-doubt that the narcissist instilled. Healing isn't just about moving on, it's about deeply understanding what happened—processing the trauma, and taking intentional steps toward emotional, mental, and even physical well-being.

Self-care, therapy, journaling, and surrounding yourself with a supportive community can all aid in this process. Setting boundaries, recognizing your triggers and reprogramming your thought patterns help in undoing the damage caused by the abuse. More importantly, healing is about giving yourself grace, there's no set timeline and setbacks don't mean failure. Every step forward, no matter how small, is a victory in reclaiming your peace and power.

> *"This is important to keep in mind that no person is completely healed. Because healing isn't linear. We go backwards and forwards and sometimes we are all over the place; but that's the process. Please don't think you need to be fully healed in order to love and good things in life."*

Self-Awareness: The First Tool for Healing

"We seek outside the wonders we carry inside us"- Rumi

This statement serves as a reminder to turn inward for answers rather than seeking them in the external world. The true sources of joy, strength, and enlightenment are already within. Self-discovery, introspection, and inner growth reveal the vast potential, wisdom and beauty we inherently possess. Fulfilment comes from with-in.

That being said- self awareness is a crucial step to healing journey. When one disconnects from self-awareness, acting out of ego, impulse, or ignorance—they become ensnared by the consequences of their own deeds.

Healing from narcissistic abuse begins with *self-awareness*—the ability to recognize your thoughts, emotions, behaviors, and patterns without judgment. It is the foundation of both psychological recovery and spiritual growth, allowing you to break free from the subconscious programming inflicted by the abuser.

It's important to identify your true self from the version of you that was created and conditioned by the narcissist. The pain and trauma you endured makes you develop certain coping mechanism and they in turn become a part of your personality over the period of time. It is important to learn that its not your authentic self—its rather temporary response to an unnatural environment than the reflection of your true self.

When you are finally out of the narcissist's grip and in the safe environment, your body, which has stored trauma for so long, slowly begins to release it. This release manifests in the form of deeply ingrained coping mechanisms that you developed for survival. As these behaviors surface, self-realization hits hard; you come to see the extent of the tragic destruction inflicted upon you and recognize that the person you became was shaped by survival, not by choice.

The release of trapped trauma isn't just psychological—it is deeply physical. Your nervous system, which had been operating in a state of hypervigilance, starts to shift, causing waves of emotional and physiological responses. You might experience sudden anxiety, unexplained fatigue, body aches, emotional outbursts, or even dissociation. The body remembers what the mind tried to suppress. As the trauma surfaces, your system works to purge it, sometimes through intense dreams, shaking, crying spells or even moments of numbness. This process is painful but necessary—your body is recalibrating itself, shedding the weight of prolonged stress and abuse, making space for healing and rediscovering who you truly are.

So how exactly do you bring self awareness? True connection with yourself comes when you turn inward, often through pain or deep experiences. The more conscious you are, the more you align with higher energy or divine guidance. This journey isn't something you control; it unfolds naturally, often in ways you least expect.

> *Observe your patterns closely; true wisdom comes from understanding your "whys." why you feel a certain way, why you act as you do, and why you repeat certain behaviors. When you uncover your "whys," you gain clarity about who you are. Knowing yourself is the biggest mystery and the greatest wisdom of all. The degree to which the person can grow is directly proportionate to the amount of truth they can handle about themselves.*

Solitude and Isolation:

What you survived is no joke! This is where spirituality comes into play. There's always a meaning and purpose behind what happens in your life and the people you meet. Every situation carries a lesson and something to learn from.

Surviving narcissistic abuse feels like a blessing—It feels like returning from a long relentless war; battered but still alive and in one piece. And the gravity of it something only you can truly understand—other people will never fully comprehend what you were made to go through. But there's definitely a spiritual element to it—a divine grace that helped you survive and make it through.

It might have already made you more attuned and aware by now. It likely pushed you to question your reality, your past, present, future over the period of years and how you ended up in this situation. Through this deep introspection within yourself, something is triggered that heightens your awareness.

The blessing in disguise is the isolation and solitude that narcissistic abuse forces upon you. Trust me, there is so much to learn in silence and solitude. By now, I'm sure you can resonate with this. Solitude becomes the key to personal growth. Someone who is deeply connected to themselves continues evolving into a better version of who they are. Solitude offers a space to simply be and observe yourself. In contrast, when surrounded by people the only voices you often hear are their opinions, unsolicited advice, and judgments. True growth begins when you take charge of your story and align it with your authentic self.

"The only way you will ever awaken is through silence"

Meditation, Breathwork, and Journaling:

Let's talk about three simple yet powerful tools that can help you on your journey—meditation, breathwork, and journaling. Don't worry, these aren't as complicated as they might sound. Let me break it down for you:

Meditation is a powerful tool for developing self-awareness and healing. By focusing all your attention, sensation or breath, meditation quiets the mind and helps you access hidden parts of yourself that are often buried under layers of pain and conditioning. As the mind slows down and consciousness expands, you can access the subconscious and superconscious parts of your field of consciousness. Through consistent meditation, you begin to see patterns in your thoughts and emotions, gaining insight into how past trauma influences your present reactions. The first step to personal growth is recognizing where you're stuck. It also opens our eyes to problems we may have been overlooking. You'll be amazed at how unshakable your determination becomes when you have a clear understanding of your values and beliefs. However, It is always better to meditate without expectation or agenda. Meditation is to connect with universal consciousness. The other experiences are all by-products.

Negative experiences in life can leave us feeling unsettled and exposed, with the emotional weight of trauma often lingering in our minds and bodies. This accumulated energy can gradually take a toll on our mental and physical well-being. Through the consistent practice of meditation, we can break free from this cycle, release the burden of pain, and restore a sense of balance and peace within ourselves.

This deepens your awareness and mindfulness, not only on a personal level but also on a broader, societal scale. It shifts your perspective on many aspects of life, often in profound ways, stripping away years of conditioning. You begin to notice faults and shortcomings not only in individuals but also in systems and patterns at a larger level. Over time, a heightened clarity emerges, allowing you to see through people's intentions and behaviors with ease. You'll feel transformed, as if a fog has lifted, revealing a sharper, clearer understanding of yourself and the world around you.

Chakra meditation is a powerful practice designed to release stuck trauma and emotions from the body by balancing and healing the body's energy centers. There are seven main chakras, each associated with specific areas of the body, emotions, and experiences. Trauma and negative emotions can create blockages in these energy centers, disrupting the natural flow of energy and causing emotional or physical discomfort.

Through chakra meditation, you focus on each chakra, using visualization, breathwork, and affirmations to clear blockages and restore balance. Starting from the root chakra, which grounds you and moving up to the crown chakra, which connects you to higher consciousness, this practice helps release suppressed emotions, dissolve tension and create harmony within the body and mind. With consistent practice, it can facilitate emotional healing, promote inner peace and allow stuck energy to flow freely once again.

Your **breath** is a powerful tool. When we're stressed or overwhelmed, we often breathe shallowly. But with intentional breathing, you can release that tension and feel more grounded. **Breath** serves as the vital connection between the body and mind, acting as a bridge that unites the physical and mental realms. It is both an unconscious function of the body and a tool that can be consciously controlled, making it a unique gateway to self-awareness. When the mind is restless or stressed, the breath often becomes shallow and erratic, reflecting the turmoil within. Conversely, by intentionally slowing and deepening the breath, one can calm the nervous system, reduce anxiety, and bring the mind into a state of clarity and focus. In practices like meditation or mindfulness, the breath anchors attention to the present moment, harmonizing the body and mind in a state of balance and awareness. This profound connection underscores the power of breath as a tool for inner peace and holistic well-being.

Journaling is like having a private conversation with yourself and it gives you clarity. When we go through challenging experiences, they can leave us feeling overwhelmed and unsettled. The emotions tied to these events often stay with us, clouding our thoughts and weighing heavily on our hearts. **Journaling** provides a powerful outlet to break free from this emotional burden. By regularly putting our thoughts and feelings into words, we can process our experiences, release the negative energy, and create space for clarity and healing.

Now how this awareness helps you change your life? Self-awareness is the cornerstone of healing, bridging the gap between your psychological wounds and your spiritual potential. By cultivating this skill, you begin to free yourself from the grip of past abuse, reconnect with your authentic self, and step into a future filled with clarity, strength, and purpose.

Self-Love

Self-love is the foundation of a healthy and fulfilling life, rooted in accepting and valuing yourself exactly as you are. It means treating yourself with kindness, compassion, and respect, just as you would a loved one. Self-love goes beyond superficial affirmations—it involves setting healthy boundaries, prioritizing your well-being, and recognizing your worth without needing external validation. By embracing self-love, you learn to let go of self-criticism and perfectionism, replacing them with patience and understanding for your growth and flaws. It empowers you to make choices aligned with your authentic self, fostering inner peace, resilience, and a deep sense of fulfillment.

Self-love means refusing to let other people's opinions define you. As a single mom navigating divorce or separation, you'll inevitably face unsolicited advice and judgments. It's crucial to not internalize these because no one has walked in your shoes. You are the best judge of your life choices and decisions, and no one has the right to criticize or overstep your boundaries. Being a single mom is incredibly challenging—you're carrying the responsibilities of two people. Remember to prioritize yourself and take breaks, regardless of what others may say. Taking care of yourself is not a luxury; it's a necessity.

Setting boundaries: Learning to say NO

Have you ever said "yes" to something and immediately regretted it?

Maybe your child's teacher asked you to take on an extra task, even though your plate was already full. Or a family member insisted you help them out, despite knowing you're juggling work, single parenting, and healing from the chaos of life after narcissistic abuse. You agreed because you didn't want to seem rude or you feared judgment. But later, as exhaustion hit, you regretted it and wondered, *Why can't I just say NO?*

If this resonates with you, it's because you've been conditioned—especially as a single mom recovering from abuse, to put others first. Narcissistic abuse trains you to neglect your own needs, to bend, and to fear conflict. Breaking free of that conditioning takes time and practice, but let me remind you: Saying "NO" is not selfish—it's survival. It's healing. It's self-love.

After dealing with a narcissist, your boundaries have likely been trampled over time and again. Your ability to say "NO" might feel rusty, even terrifying but it's crucial. If you are a single mom, you're not just responsible for yourself, you're also creating a healthy and stable environment for your child. Learning to say "NO" isn't just for your benefit—it's for theirs too.

Setting healthy boundaries and learning to say "NO" are essential components of self-care. Boundaries are not walls that separate us from others but rather a way to define what is acceptable and what is not in our relationships and interactions. Saying "NO" is a powerful act of self-respect, allowing us to protect our energy, time and emotional well-being. It is about honoring your own needs and values instead of sacrificing them to please others or avoid discomfort. When we learn to say "NO" confidently, we create space for the things that truly matter to us and align with our priorities.

The importance of saying "NO" lies in its ability to set limits that ensure balance in our lives. Often, we overcommit ourselves out of fear of rejection, guilt, or the desire to be seen as helpful. However, constantly saying "yes" when we genuinely want to say "NO" can lead to feelings of resentment, burnout and a loss of personal identity. When we stretch ourselves too thin, we compromise our ability to care for ourselves, which ultimately affects our ability to show up for others in a meaningful way. Saying "no" is not selfish—it is an act of self-preservation and an acknowledgment that your time and energy are finite.

Failing to say "NO" when we need to can have long-term consequences on our mental, emotional, and even physical health. Suppressing our true feelings to accommodate others often creates inner conflict, leading to anxiety, stress and even feelings of powerlessness. It can also damage relationships, as unspoken frustrations build up over time, eventually leading to emotional outbursts or complete disengagement. By not setting boundaries, we unintentionally teach others that it's acceptable to overlook our needs or take advantage of our willingness, creating unhealthy dynamics.

Learning to say "NO" is an act of self-love and self-respect. It helps us maintain our integrity and reminds us that our needs and well-being matter just as much as anyone else's. While it may feel uncomfortable at first, especially if you're not used to setting boundaries, practicing saying "NO" in a kind but firm way can be liberating. Remember, every "NO" to something that drains you is a "YES" to yourself and the things that bring you peace, joy, and fulfilment.

Physical exercise: Trauma Release

Physical exercise is a form of self- love. It's a way of taking care of your body, mind, and soul. Whether it's going for a run, practicing yoga, or lifting weights, every movement is a gift to yourself—helping you grow stronger, feel healthier, and connect with yourself on a deeper level. **It's not just about aesthetics—it's about respecting and honoring the vessel that carries you through life.**

Trauma is deeply embedded in the physical body often residing in the tissues, muscles, and fascia long after the mind has consciously processed the experience. The physical body has an extraordinary capacity to store memory, estimated to be trillions of times more than the mental body. Every emotional wound, stressor, or traumatic event leaves an imprint, altering the body's cellular memory and creating a somatic response. While the mind processes thoughts and events in a linear way, the body absorbs and retains sensations, energy, and patterns on a cellular level. Every cell in the body carries imprints of our past—be it joy, pain, or unresolved emotions, which can manifest physically through tension, posture, or even illness. This is why people often feel tightness, spasm and pain, or unexplained discomfort in certain areas of their body, even when they are unaware of the emotional roots. The body remembers, even when the mind tries to forget, highlighting the intricate connection between the physical and emotional realms. Healing from trauma often requires not just mental work but also addressing these physical imprints through modalities like somatic therapy, yoga, breathwork, or movement practices. They help unlock and release what the mind may not even be aware of.

Physical exercise plays a vital role in releasing trauma stored in the body by facilitating **somatic release**, a process where unresolved emotional pain and stress trapped in the tissues and nervous system are discharged. Trauma often creates a "freeze" response in the body, leaving it in a state of hypervigilance or tension. Movement helps break this cycle by activating the parasympathetic nervous system, which promotes relaxation and safety. Activities like yoga, dance, or even shaking allow the body to complete movements or responses that were suppressed during the original traumatic event.

Somatic release happens when the body is given permission to reconnect with its sensations without judgment. For example, deep breathing during exercise oxygenates the tissues, encouraging relaxation, while stretching or rhythmic movements release tension stored in muscles and fascia. Exercises like running or boxing help release pent-up aggression or fear, while practices like yoga encourage mindfulness, allowing the body and mind to integrate the experience. Over time, these practices reset the nervous system and create space for healing, replacing the memory of trauma with a sense of safety and vitality.

Art and Hobbies as Therapy

Hobbies and art play a significant role in healing by offering a creative outlet to process emotions, reconnect with joy, and rebuild a sense of self that may have been lost through trauma. Engaging in creative activities, such as painting, drawing, writing, knitting, gardening, or playing a musical instrument, allows individuals to express emotions that are often too overwhelming or complex to verbalize. This nonverbal expression bypasses the analytical mind and taps directly into the subconscious, where trauma is often stored.

Art, in particular acts as a bridge between the inner world and outer expression. For instance, sketching, painting, or sculpting provides a safe and tactile way to externalize pain, anger, or grief. The act of creating something beautiful or meaningful from chaos can be deeply therapeutic, as it transforms emotional turmoil into something **tangible**, offering a sense of control and resolution. Art therapy, a guided practice, focuses on this concept by helping individuals use creativity to explore and release buried emotions.

Hobbies, on the other hand, encourage playfulness, curiosity, and presence. They help shift focus away from ruminating thoughts and reawaken a sense of purpose and passion. Activities like gardening or cooking are grounding and meditative, while hobbies like dancing or singing encourage emotional release through movement and sound. Pursuing a hobby also fosters mindfulness, helping individuals stay anchored in the present moment and reducing feelings of anxiety or dissociation.

Furthermore, hobbies and art promote neuroplasticity—the brain's ability to form new neural connections. Creating something new, whether it's a painting or a garden bed, rewires the brain to associate positive emotions with the activity, gradually replacing negative patterns created by trauma. It also builds self-esteem, as completing a project, mastering a skill, or simply enjoying the process can reignite feelings of accomplishment and self-worth.

Ultimately, art and hobbies reconnect individuals with their sense of identity and individuality. They remind us that healing isn't just about processing pain but also about rediscovering joy, passion, and creativity; essential components of a fulfilling and resilient life.

Acceptance and Surrender

As a survivor of over a decade of narcissistic abuse, I've often found myself grappling with the question, "**Why me**?" It's a question that haunts many survivors, especially in the early stages of healing. Why did I have to endure this pain? What did I do to deserve this? The truth is, these questions are natural—but they can also trap you in a cycle of self-blame and despair.

The reality is that narcissistic abuse says nothing about your **worth** or who you are as a person. It reflects the abuser's deeply rooted flaws and dysfunction. Their manipulation and cruelty were never your fault. Recognizing this truth is the first step toward letting go—not only of the pain but also of the need to find all the answers.

Letting go is a concept that I've never truly connected with in the way it's often described. For me, the journey of healing begins with *acceptance* and *surrender*—fully embracing the reality of the situation and allowing myself to feel every emotion tied to it. I believe that true healing comes **not** from pushing feelings aside or **forcing** ourselves to "**let go**," but from processing them deeply and giving them the attention they deserve.

Whether it's grief, sadness, anger, or even joy, every emotion carries energy that needs to move through us. When we suppress these emotions or rush to let them go, we only prolong their hold on us. Instead, I've found that the most profound transformations happen when we surrender to the feeling. We allow ourselves to sit with it, to acknowledge its presence.

Surrendering to emotions doesn't mean wallowing in them indefinitely. It's about creating space for those feelings to exist without judgment. It's about telling yourself, "I feel this way right now, and that's okay." This acceptance allows the emotion to flow through you rather than getting stuck inside, manifesting as anxiety, numbness or despair.

Once the emotion has been processed—fully felt and acknowledged, the next step is transformation. Every feeling, no matter how painful, carries a message or a lesson. What can this experience teach me? What has this emotion revealed about myself, my boundaries, or my desires? This stage isn't about rationalizing the abuse or justifying someone else's actions. It's about extracting meaning for your own growth and resilience.

For example, grief might teach us about the depth of our love and capacity for connection. Anger can show us where our boundaries were crossed and why they matter. Even sadness can illuminate what truly matters to us. Transformation comes when we take these lessons and allow them to shape us into someone stronger, wiser, and more attuned to our own needs.

In my view, healing is not about "letting go" in the traditional sense—it's about **embracing** first. It's about meeting yourself where you are, allowing the full range of human emotions to exist, and then channeling those feelings into wisdom and growth. When you approach healing this way, you don't force yourself to move on **prematurely**. Instead, you naturally reach a point where the emotions no longer weigh you down because you've processed and **transformed** them into stepping stones for your journey forward.

Acceptance and surrender are acts of self-love. They are the foundation for healing, growth, and ultimately, freedom. You reclaim your power not by forgetting the past, but by fully feeling and learning from it.

> *"Emotional trauma doesn't fade with time, heal on its own, or make us stronger. Its not something we rush to "heal" in pursuit of feeling whole, loved or accepted. In stead, emotional trauma is what we meet with everything that was once absent – acknowledgment, attunement, presence, love, and infinite patience. The meeting is the healing."*

> *"A person who doesn't suppress what they feel and can gently be present to their inner ups and downs will have a foundation of inner maturity."- Yung Pueblo*

Healing the Nervous System

The nervous system doesn't differentiate between people when it comes to its needs—it responds to how those needs are met or unmet. If you acknowledge and meet your own nervous system's needs—like feeling seen, safe, and validated; you reduce dependence on others for these feelings. This creates internal stability and safety, which is essential for emotional well-being.

Telling a traumatized person to "let it go" invalidates their lived experience and the responses of their nervous system. Triggers are not a sign of unwillingness but a reflection of unresolved trauma stored in the body. Healing requires understanding and support, not dismissal.

Your nervous system heals in stillness, your gut health heals in gentleness, your hormones heal in nourishment. Showing your body some grace and compassion is the deepest medicine.

Your nervous system heals in slowness, putting pressure on yourself to heal will lead to the dysregulated nervous system which eventually leads to physical illnesses such as hormonal imbalance, autoimmune diseases.

"Heal!! Your mother may never apologize, trapped in her belief that she acted righteously. Your father may never acknowledge his wrongs, blinded by his own sense of righteousness. Family members may never take responsibility, trapped in the same cycle of toxicity they are yet to break. That sibling or best friend may never express regret for not being there for you, and that friend may never feel guilt for invalidating your experience. Betrayal often comes from those closest to us and their inability to feel remorse or take accountability can cut the deepest.

Even the legal system or support services may never apologize for failing you, unaware of the impact of their inaction.

But remember their inability to heal, apologize or change does not define your worth. Heal for yourself—not because they deserve your forgiveness or closure but because you deserve peace. You owe it to your journey to rise above the pain."

Building resilience: Reclaiming Your Identity

Resilience is not just about surviving narcissistic abuse—it's about rediscovering the person you were before the manipulation, gaslighting, and control took hold. Narcissistic abuse leaves you feeling disconnected from yourself, unsure of your own thoughts, feelings, and decisions. Reclaiming your identity is a process of undoing the false reality that was forced upon you and rebuilding yourself from the inside out.

At its core, resilience is the ability to rise from emotional devastation with a stronger sense of self. It is not about suppressing pain or pretending to be unaffected but about embracing your experiences, learning from them, and using them as fuel for transformation.This is about shifting from a state of survival to a place where you truly own your story and reclaim your power.

The journey to resilience is deeply personal. It is about confronting the lies you were made to believe about your worth, your intelligence, your abilities and replacing them with your own truth. It is about recognizing that your identity is not defined by the abuse but by the strength it took to break free.

Reclaiming yourself means allowing joy, trust, and self-expression back into your life. It means finding comfort in your own presence, making decisions without fear, and redefining success on your own terms. Most importantly, it is about realizing that you are not broken—you are evolving into someone who is wiser, more aware and unshakably strong.

True resilience is not just about bouncing back—it's about bouncing forward, toward a life where you are no longer a victim of your past but the author of your future.

CHAPTER 14

BEYOND SURVIVAL: FROM PAIN TO PREVENTION

Narcissistic abuse leaves more than just visible scars—it reshapes the way survivors see themselves, relationships, and the world around them. The aftermath is often filled with confusion, suppressed anger, and a deep sense of betrayal, especially when faced with the realization that many connections were never real to begin with. Society's misconceptions about narcissistic abuse only add to the struggle, making it harder for survivors to validate their experiences and distinguish truth from manipulation.

The best way to protect yourself from narcissistic abuse is to recognize the warning signs before you become deeply entangled. While many survivors look back and see the red flags they ignored, awareness in the early stages can prevent emotional and psychological harm. This chapter focuses on early detection—subtle behaviors that indicate narcissistic tendencies, how to differentiate between genuine affection and manipulation, and the importance of trusting your instincts.

Supressed Anger After Narcissistic Abuse

If you're a survivor or currently going through it, you know exactly what I'm talking about. I see you, and I feel you. There's so much suppressed anger, isn't there? The anger for every little thing they sabotaged. For everything you loved and worked for that they destroyed. For how they *assassinated your character* because they couldn't defeat you any other way. For turning your family and friends against you, alienating your child, or even manipulating the legal system to gain control. With a narcissist, it feels like you lose **everything**, most importantly your spirit and that anger just sits there, heavy and unresolved.

But let's be honest; what could you do with that anger while you were in the thick of it? There was no room for it. You were too busy surviving. Too busy walking on eggshells, managing their outbursts or protecting yourself and your child. Expressing your anger would have only given them ammunition to twist it against you, more gaslighting, more isolation, more chaos. So the anger stayed hidden, bottled up inside. But just because it's suppressed doesn't mean it's gone. No, it stays with you. It turns inward, morphing into shame, anxiety or guilt. It whispers lies like, *Maybe I am too sensitive. Maybe I didn't do enough. Maybe it was my fault.* You feel it, don't you? That unspoken, simmering rage that eats away at your peace.

Here's the truth you need to hear: That anger is valid. It's not something to hide or be ashamed of. It's a natural, *human* response to **injustice**. It's your mind and body screaming, *What happened to me was wrong.* That anger is there because your experiences *mattered*.

Allow yourself to acknowledge the anger. it's time to let it out. Not for them, for *you*. Write it down, name it. Journal every thought, every betrayal, every injustice. Say it out loud in a safe space—therapy, a support group, even a trusted friend. Scream into a pillow. Cry in the shower. Punch the air if you need to. Whatever it takes, give yourself permission to feel. Suppressed anger doesn't heal on its own—it needs an outlet.

Anger, when processed, becomes a force for transformation. It teaches you boundaries—it's your internal alarm that says, *I will never tolerate this again.* It reminds you that your pain was real, that your experience matters, and that you deserve better. Suppressed anger doesn't define you but when you release it, it can liberate you. It's not about staying stuck in the rage—it's about moving through it to reach clarity, peace, and ultimately, freedom.

> *Anger isn't something to eliminate, suppress or act out impulsively.*
> *Instead, it evolves when we recognize and honor its underlying needs.*

What does anger truly need? To be acknowledged, understood and expressed authentically in its original form.

Misconceptions about narcissistic abuse

There are Many misconceptions surrounding narcissistic abuse, and one of the most common is that people often equate it with typical relationship conflicts or misunderstandings. Unlike normal disagreements between couples, narcissistic abuse is rooted in manipulation, control, and a deliberate pattern of emotional harm.

Many believe that narcissistic abuse is similar to the usual ups and downs of a relationship, where couples may have disagreements or emotional conflicts. However, narcissistic abuse is much more **insidious**. It involves psychological manipulation, gaslighting, and emotional exploitation, all designed to undermine the victim's sense of self-worth and reality. Unlike normal conflicts, this form of abuse isn't just a result of miscommunication—it's a calculated pattern of control that can be hard for outsiders to detect.

Both people must be responsible for the abuse

Another misconception is the belief that the victim must have done something to provoke the abuser's behavior. People sometimes assume that abuse occurs as a response to something the victim did. In narcissistic abuse, the victim often does nothing to trigger the abuser's behavior. Narcissists are often motivated by their own insecurities, desire for control, and lack of empathy. Their abusive behavior is not a reaction but a choice to manipulate and dominate others.

Narcissistic abuse only involves emotional manipulation

While emotional manipulation is a hallmark of narcissistic abuse, many overlook that it can include multiple types of abuse: psychological, verbal, financial, and even physical abuse. Narcissists often use a wide range of tactics to control their victims, from isolation to financial dependence. The abuse can manifest in subtle ways, leaving the victim feeling confused and trapped.

It's obvious to outsiders

A significant misconception is that narcissistic abuse should be obvious to others. In reality, narcissists are experts at maintaining a charismatic, likable public persona while privately tormenting their victims. The abuse is often subtle, insidious, and slow to develop, making it difficult for friends, family, or even the victim themselves to recognize until the damage is done. This makes narcissistic abuse particularly isolating.

Narcissists can change if they find the right person

Some people believe that a narcissist can change if they are with someone who "loves them enough" or "understands them." In truth, narcissistic personality disorder (NPD) is a deeply ingrained psychological condition that is extremely resistant to change. While therapy might help manage some behaviors, it often requires a significant level of self-awareness, which narcissists typically lack.

Leaving a narcissist is easy

Many assume that leaving a narcissistic relationship is straightforward, but it's often far from it. Narcissists use tactics like gaslighting, love-bombing and trauma bonding to create deep emotional dependencies, making it very hard for the victim to break free. Additionally, after leaving, victims may face ongoing manipulation, such as stalking or attempts to sabotage their new life.

These misconceptions can make it even harder for survivors of narcissistic abuse to seek help or be taken seriously. Raising awareness about the complexity and subtlety of narcissistic abuse is crucial in helping survivors feel understood and supported.

Preventing Narcissistic Abuse: Understanding the Red Flags

Prevention begins with awareness. Narcissists often start with charm, charisma and calculated kindness that can feel intoxicating at first. But beneath the surface, there are always signs: excessive need for admiration, lack of empathy, and a tendency to manipulate or control. Pay attention to how someone reacts when you set boundaries or express a need—they may reveal their true colors when their sense of entitlement is challenged. The earlier you recognize these red flags, the better you can avoid falling into their web.

1. Building Strong Boundaries

Boundaries are your first line of defense against narcissistic abuse. They protect your mental and emotional well-being and send a clear message: "I respect myself, and I won't allow anyone to cross this line." A narcissist will test your boundaries early, often in subtle ways, such as dismissing your feelings, making "jokes" at your expense or violating your time and energy. Standing firm and enforcing boundaries consistently is critical to discouraging further attempts at control.

2. Cultivating Self-Worth

Narcissists often prey on individuals with low self-esteem or those who are people-pleasers. They thrive on exploiting insecurities and making you doubt yourself. Prevention lies in strengthening your sense of self-worth and understanding that your value is not tied to how others perceive or treat you. When you operate from a place of self-love and confidence, narcissists have less power to manipulate you.

3. Trusting Your Instincts

Your intuition is one of your strongest allies. If something feels off, it probably is. Narcissists are masters of creating confusion and making you second-guess yourself through gaslighting. Learning to trust your instincts, even in the absence of "proof," can help you avoid dangerous situations. Remember, you don't need to justify your discomfort to anyone.

4. Educating Yourself About Narcissistic Traits

Prevention often stems from understanding. The more you know about narcissistic behaviors; like love bombing, devaluation, and discarding, the easier it becomes to spot their patterns. This knowledge empowers you to identify toxic relationships before they escalate and equips you to disengage from potential abusers without falling for their manipulations.

5. Surrounding Yourself with Supportive Relationships

A strong support network acts as a buffer against manipulation. Narcissists isolate their victims, but when you maintain healthy connections with people who genuinely care about you, it becomes harder for a narcissist to control you. Seek relationships that are built on mutual respect, trust, and kindness—these are the people who will stand by you when red flags appear.

6. Practicing Emotional Detachment

Prevention isn't just about avoiding a narcissist but also about controlling how much power they have over your emotions. By practicing emotional detachment, you create a buffer between their behavior and your well-being. Techniques like the grey rock method, mindfulness, or simply limiting interactions can prevent their toxic energy from infiltrating your peace.

7. Recognizing Your Own Patterns

Lastly, prevention also involves self-reflection. Are you drawn to people who mirror narcissistic tendencies because of past experiences? Do you ignore red flags in the hope that someone will change? Identifying your own patterns and healing unresolved wounds can reduce the chances of repeating toxic cycles.

How to Identify the True Victim vs. the Narcissist: Key Signs

Distinguish between the true victim and the narcissist:

1. **Look for Consistency in Behavior:**

   o   The victim often shows consistent distress, anxiety, or confusion in their emotions and actions.

   o   The narcissist tends to have a charming, composed, or even "perfect" demeanor in public but may lash out or manipulate in private.

2. **Watch for Accountability:**

   o   Victims often question themselves, blame themselves, or try to find solutions, even if they shouldn't feel responsible.

   o   Narcissists rarely take accountability and instead blame the victim for everything, projecting their own faults outward.

3. **Observe Patterns in Storytelling:**

   o   Victims tend to share experiences that reveal their pain or the harm caused to them, often with hesitation or fear of being misunderstood.

   o   Narcissists will focus on discrediting the other person, often exaggerating their victimhood and portraying themselves as completely blameless.

4. **Empathy as a Marker:**

   o   Victims often try to understand the abuser's actions or justify them, showing an emotional depth and empathy for others.

   o   Narcissists lack genuine empathy and may instead show performative concern or use emotional manipulation to gain favor.

5. **How They Handle Control:**

   o   Victims typically try to regain control over their own lives and are exhausted from walking on eggshells.

   o   Narcissists seek to control others—whether through overt dominance or covert manipulation; and show resistance to losing that power.

6. **Body Language and Energy:**

   o   Victims often appear drained, nervous, or on edge, even when talking about seemingly small things.

   o   Narcissists usually radiate confidence or arrogance, with body language that demands attention, admiration or charm.

7. **Seeking Therapy as a Clue:**

   o   Victims are more likely to seek therapy or external support as they try to process their trauma, heal, and regain clarity. They focus on self-improvement and are open to working on themselves.

   o   Narcissists rarely seek therapy, and if they do, it's often to manipulate the narrative, play the victim, or avoid accountability. They may also use therapy as a tool to gaslight the victim further.

The willingness to seek genuine help and take responsibility for personal healing is a strong indicator of who the true victim is. By observing these subtle but significant behaviors, you can better understand who is genuinely suffering and who is perpetuating the harm.

The Strength in Choosing Solitude Over Fake Connections

Have you noticed how society often operates on a foundation of strategic niceness and inorganic positivity? People practice kindness as a performance, offering shallow pleasantries that lack depth or sincerity. It's not real connection—it's a show, a way to maintain appearances to seem like a good person while avoiding the discomfort of authenticity.

When you've been through the storm of narcissistic abuse or any life-altering pain, you begin to see through this façade. You recognize the fake smiles, the empty encouragement, and the forced positivity that doesn't allow space for real emotions or struggles. And let's not forget the people who strategically insert themselves into your life, offering conditional support that evaporates the moment it's inconvenient for them.

The truth is, the strength it takes to walk away from these surface-level connections to choose solitude over poorly surrounding yourself is vastly underrated. **Society doesn't talk enough about this strength because it's hard to glorify something that doesn't look pretty or easy. But let me tell you—choosing to be alone, to sit with your own company is one of the bravest things you can do.**

Why? Because being alone forces you to face yourself, to confront the pain, the healing, and the growth that fake connections only distract you from. It takes courage to say, **I would rather sit in my truth than surround myself with people who invalidate it.** It takes resilience to choose authenticity over the comfort of blending in with a crowd that doesn't truly see you.

When you remove the toxic positivity and the fake kindness, you realize just how much noise they create—noise that drowns out your own voice, your own needs, and your own healing. Solitude, on the other hand, gives you clarity. **It teaches you to rely on yourself, to validate your own worth, and to find peace in your own presence.**

This doesn't mean you'll be alone forever. But when you rebuild, you'll be selective. You'll no longer tolerate half-hearted connections or strategic kindness that serves others more than it serves you. You'll choose relationships that feel like safety, not performance.

So, if you're sitting in solitude right now, know this: **you're not weak.** You're not isolated because something is wrong with you. You're strong because you chose peace over pretense. You chose to prioritize your self-worth over shallow connections. And that choice? It's not just brave, it's transformative.

In a world that encourages you to settle for "good enough," choosing solitude is a quiet rebellion, a radical act of self-love. Hold on to that strength, because it's leading you to the life and the connections you truly deserve.

The Call for Kindness: Don't Turn a Blind Eye

Abuse thrives in silence. It gains strength when we look away, when we choose not to get involved, or when we dismiss someone's struggle as "not our problem." But for those enduring abuse or struggling with mental health challenges, this silence can feel like abandonment. They often carry their pain in isolation, longing for someone to see them, to believe them and to remind them they are not alone.

If you ever suspect that someone is being abused or struggling mentally, please don't turn a blind eye. Your kindness, your acknowledgment and your support could be the very thing that saves them. Abuse is not always obvious and mental health struggles are often hidden but a genuine act of compassion—whether offering help, listening without judgment, or simply being present, can make all the difference.

One harsh remark can drive a victim of narcissistic abuse toward devastating actions, while one act of kindness or a thoughtful word can offer them a lifeline. Living with narcissistic abuse feels like being slowly torn apart, bit by bit, until there's nothing left. If you've never experienced it, understand that your words carry weight. You could unknowingly push someone closer to ending their life, or you could save them from the brink. Be kind; your words might be the reason someone chooses to keep fighting.

Please don't turn a blind eye. Be kind. Be compassionate! And if you can help, do it.

CHAPTER 15

RAISING A TRAUMA FREE GENERATION

Breaking free from narcissistic abuse is not just about personal healing—it's about ensuring that future generations do not inherit these cycles of trauma, manipulation, and emotional neglect. When children witness narcissistic abuse, they internalize these dynamics, leading them to either tolerate mistreatment or unconsciously adopt similar behaviors. The responsibility of cycle-breaking rests on those who recognize these toxic patterns and take intentional steps to raise emotionally secure and resilient children. This chapter explores the practical steps needed to foster a trauma-free upbringing, ensuring that children grow up feeling safe, valued, and emotionally whole.

Breaking Generational Trauma

Tragically, narcissism is a toxic legacy that often passes through generations, shaping dysfunctional family dynamics. A dysregulated mother may instill narcissistic traits in her son, who then carries forward the cycle of abuse with his own children. Even those who escape developing NPD themselves may unknowingly gravitate toward narcissistic partners, further entrenching the cycle. This ripple effect creates a generational chain of emotional dysfunction, where patterns of control, manipulation, and trauma continue to thrive unless consciously broken.

But generational trauma does not have to be a life sentence. Survivors of narcissistic abuse have the power to disrupt this cycle by becoming aware of these patterns and making intentional choices in how they raise their children. The key to breaking free lies in **self-awareness, emotional regulation, and conscious parenting.**

1. **Lead by Example: Healing Starts with You**
   Children learn more from what they see than what they are told. If they witness a parent setting firm boundaries, walking away from toxic situations, and prioritizing self-care, they internalize these behaviors as normal. Breaking the cycle begins with unlearning harmful conditioning and modeling the kind of self-respect and emotional security you want your child to develop.

2. **Foster Open Communication and Emotional Intelligence**
   Children need to feel safe expressing their emotions without fear of punishment or dismissal. Encouraging open dialogue, validating their feelings and teaching them to identify and regulate emotions helps them build self-trust. Emotionally intelligent children grow into adults who can recognize manipulation and refuse to tolerate toxic behaviors.

3. **Teach Healthy Boundaries and the Power of 'No'**
   Narcissistic households condition children to prioritize others at their own expense. Teaching kids that their needs, feelings and personal space matter prevents them from becoming people-pleasers or falling into exploitative relationships. Allow them to say "no" without guilt and respect their choices, reinforcing that their voice is valuable.

4. **Help Them Recognize Manipulation Early**
   Rather than simply warning children about "bad people," educate them on specific manipulation tactics- gaslighting, guilt-tripping, love-bombing and coercion, in an age-appropriate way. When they understand these patterns early, they are less likely to be deceived by toxic individuals in friendships, romantic relationships, or professional settings.

5. **Encourage Independent Thinking Over Blind Obedience**
   Narcissistic environments demand compliance and discourage critical thinking. Instead of teaching children to obey without question, encourage curiosity and decision-making. Let them analyze situations, form their own opinions, and understand that they are allowed to challenge unfair authority. This strengthens their ability to resist control and stand firm in their values.

6. **Build a Strong Support System**
   Isolation makes individuals vulnerable to abuse. Teaching children to seek out and maintain healthy, supportive relationships; whether through friends, mentors, or trusted adults—ensures they have a network to rely on outside of the immediate family. A strong support system helps them develop confidence and independence.

7. **Strengthen Their Self-Worth and Self-Validation**
   One of the most damaging effects of narcissistic abuse is an ingrained need for external validation. Children should grow up knowing that their worth is not dependent on achievements, social status, or the approval of others. Encouraging self-acceptance, resilience, and inner confidence ensures they don't seek validation from manipulative people later in life.

8. **Shield Them from Toxic Family Influence**
   Even after escaping a narcissistic relationship, toxic relatives such as narcissistic grandparents or flying monkeys—can continue to undermine your parenting. Establish firm boundaries, limit exposure when necessary, and teach your child how to recognize and disengage from manipulative behaviors within the family.

9. **Teach Healthy Conflict Resolution**
   Growing up in a narcissistic household often means experiencing either excessive conflict or complete avoidance of it. Teaching children how to handle disagreements with respect, listen to different perspectives,

and express their needs without fear instills confidence in dealing with difficult people and situations.

As survivors, we have the ability to rewrite the narrative—not just for ourselves, but for the next generation. By raising children who are emotionally secure, self-aware, and resilient, we break the chain of **dysfunction** and ensure that abuse does not continue to thrive in our lineage. Of course we cannot guarantee what they will encounter in the future or how life will shape them, but we can equip them with the tools to navigate it. By instilling self-worth, emotional awareness and the ability to recognize abuse in any form, we give them the best possible defense against toxicity. They may still face challenges, but they will know who they are, what they deserve, and how to stand firm in their truth and that in itself is a victory.

Ensuring a Trauma-Free Generation

Breaking generational trauma is not just about avoiding past mistakes—it's about actively building a foundation of emotional safety, self-awareness, and resilience. To raise a trauma-free generation, we must go beyond identifying toxic patterns and take conscious steps to nurture a healthier emotional environment.

1. **Cultivating Emotional Security from Infancy**
   A child's first experience with safety and trust begins at home. Responsive parenting—meeting emotional and physical needs without dismissing or neglecting them, creates a secure attachment. A child who knows they are valued and heard grows up with emotional stability, making them less susceptible to future trauma.

2. **Redefining Discipline as Guidance, Not Control**
   Harsh discipline, including verbal humiliation, excessive punishment, or authoritarian parenting, fosters fear rather than respect. Instead of demanding obedience, focus on teaching accountability through open discussions, natural consequences and problem-solving strategies.

Children learn best when they understand why certain behaviors are encouraged or discouraged.

3. **Encouraging Emotional Resilience Over Suppression**
   Instead of teaching children to "toughen up" or "move on" without processing emotions, help them understand that emotions are natural. Provide them with tools to manage stress, disappointment and setbacks without resorting to avoidance, self-blame or emotional detachment. Resilient children become emotionally intelligent adults who can navigate life's hardships without internalizing trauma.

4. **Creating an Environment of Unconditional Acceptance**
   Many children raised in narcissistic or high-conflict households grow up believing that love is *conditional*—tied to performance, compliance, or pleasing others. Reinforce that their worth is not based on achievements or meeting external expectations but on who they are as individuals. *A child who feels accepted at home does not seek validation in toxic relationships.*

5. **Normalizing Emotional Regulation and Self-Reflection**
   Children mirror their caregivers' emotional responses. If they witness reactive outbursts, silent treatment or emotional neglect, they internalize these as normal coping mechanisms. Demonstrating self-awareness, pausing before reacting and openly discussing feelings teaches them that emotions are manageable, not overwhelming forces to fear or suppress.

6. **Providing a Safe Space for Exploration and Identity Development**
   Generational trauma often stems from rigid expectations, where children are pressured to fit predetermined roles. Instead, allow them to explore their interests, form their own beliefs, and develop a sense of self without guilt or shame. A trauma-free upbringing encourages autonomy and personal growth rather than compliance and fear of failure.

7. **Addressing Generational Wounds Within Ourselves**
    We cannot break the cycle if we continue to carry unhealed wounds.
    Seeking therapy, self-reflection, and learning new parenting approaches
    ensures that we do not unconsciously project our unresolved trauma onto
    the next generation. Healing is not just about breaking patterns— it's
    about rewriting the story from a place of awareness and empowerment.

By fostering emotional security, autonomy and self-worth, we move beyond
merely stopping toxic cycles—we actively build a future where children grow
up feeling safe, valued, and empowered. A trauma-free generation is not an
unattainable dream but a conscious commitment we make every day in how
we show up, parent, and heal.

Conscious Parenting

1. **Practicing Presence Over Perfection**
    Many parents, especially those breaking generational trauma, feel
    immense pressure to parent perfectly. However, children don't need
    perfection—they need presence. Being emotionally available, listening
    without distractions, and validating their experiences creates a secure
    bond. Even when mistakes happen, repairing the connection through open
    communication teaches them that relationships can be safe and forgiving.

2. **Teaching Self-Compassion Alongside Self-Discipline**
    Children often internalize their parents' self-talk. If they witness harsh
    self-criticism, they may develop the same inner dialogue. Teaching them
    that mistakes are opportunities for learning, rather than failures that
    define worth, fosters self-compassion. Encouraging self-discipline should
    never come at the cost of self-worth.

3. **Recognizing and Respecting Neurodiversity**
    Every child processes emotions and information differently. Understanding
    neurodivergence (ADHD, autism, high sensitivity, etc.) helps tailor

parenting approaches to fit the child's needs, rather than forcing them into a neurotypical mold. A trauma-free upbringing acknowledges and accommodates individual differences with patience and understanding.

4. **Strengthening the Parent-Child Relationship Before Correcting Behaviour**

   Traditional parenting often prioritizes obedience over connection. Instead of using punishment as the first response, seek to understand the root cause of misbehaviour. Connection before correction builds trust, ensuring that discipline guides rather than instils fear. When children feel understood, they are more open to learning accountability in a healthy way.

5. **Encouraging Play and Creativity as Emotional Expression**

   Play is a child's natural way of processing emotions and making sense of the world. Providing unstructured playtime, creative outlets and nature-based activities fosters emotional intelligence and problem-solving skills. Suppressing playfulness in childhood often leads to emotional repression in adulthood.

6. **Raising Emotionally Safe Siblings**

   If there are multiple children in the family, preventing sibling trauma is crucial. Favoritism, comparisons, or pitting siblings against each other create deep-seated wounds. Teaching conflict resolution, emphasizing teamwork over competition and ensuring each child feels equally valued nurtures healthy sibling bonds that last into adulthood.

7. **Preparing Them for a World That Isn't Always Safe**

   While we strive to create emotionally safe homes, the outside world won't always reflect the same values. Teaching children about healthy skepticism, self-advocacy, and recognizing unsafe situations ensures they can navigate challenges without falling into harmful patterns. A trauma-free generation isn't just sheltered from harm—it is equipped to handle life with confidence and self-awareness.

8. **Modeling Emotional Repair and Healthy Apologies**
   Children who grow up in environments where conflicts are never resolved or apologies are rare struggle with emotional closure. Demonstrating genuine apologies, taking responsibility for mistakes and working toward solutions teaches them that relationships can be safe, even when conflicts arise.

Lets build a world where children grow,
Free from pain they'll never know
Where love is pure, not just a game,
And no small heart is burned by shame.
No silent cries behind closed doors,
No tiny hands that beg for more.
No fear of love that twists and bends,
No trust betrayed by those called friends.
Let's teach them strength, lets teach them grace,
Let them bloom in a safer place.
A world where scars don't shape their way,
But light and love will lead the day.

AFTER THOUGHT

Empowering Reflection

As you reach the end of this book, I want to invite you to take a moment to reflect—not just on the words you've read, but on yourself. The fact that you picked up this book and stayed with it is a testament to your courage and strength. It's not easy to face the realities of narcissistic abuse, let alone explore your own patterns, vulnerabilities, and healing journey.

Think about the person you were before you began reading and the awareness you now hold. What have you learned about yourself? About your relationships? About the dynamics that have shaped your life? Every chapter you've read is a step toward reclaiming your power, your self-worth and your voice.

You are more resilient than you may realize. Whether you've just started to understand the cycle of abuse or are actively working toward breaking free, each effort you make—no matter how small, matters. Every time you recognize a red flag, honor a boundary or choose yourself over toxicity, you're rewriting your story.

This reflection isn't about perfection or having all the answers. It's about celebrating your decision to seek truth, to grow and to prioritize your well-being. **You've already begun a journey that many fear to start, and that alone is a sign of your strength.**

So, pause here. Take a deep breath. Acknowledge how far you've come, and hold onto the hope of where you're headed. This book is just one tool in your healing, but the real work and the real transformation, lies within you. You have everything you need to build a life filled with peace, clarity and freedom.

There will be days when anxiety creeps in, when self-doubt tries to take over or when the weight of everything feels unbearable. **In those moments, your breath is your power.**

Here are some simple breathing exercises you can turn to whenever you need **calm, clarity or emotional balance.**

1. **Box Breathing – Regaining a Sense of Control**

    o **When to use:** In moments of panic, emotional overwhelm or when you feel like everything is spiraling out of control.

    o **Why it works:** Box breathing slows the heart rate, relaxes the nervous system and restores balance—perfect for when anxiety feels unbearable.

    How to do it:

    1. Inhale deeply through your nose for 4 seconds.

    2. Hold your breath for 4 seconds.

    3. Exhale slowly through your mouth for 4 seconds.

    4. Hold again for 4 seconds.

    5. Repeat this cycle for a few minutes.

Imagine drawing a box with each breath—this visualization helps ground you in the present moment.

2. **4-7-8 Breathing – Releasing Stored Anxiety**

    o **When to use:** If your mind won't stop racing, you struggle with sleep or you're overwhelmed by intrusive thoughts.

- **Why it works:** By extending the exhale, this technique activates the parasympathetic nervous system, calming the body and mind.

How to do it:

1. Inhale through your nose for 4 seconds.

2. Hold your breath for 7 seconds.

3. Exhale slowly through your mouth for 8 seconds.

4. Repeat 4-5 times.

If holding for 7 seconds feels difficult, shorten it. The key is making your exhale longer than your inhale, which tells your brain that you are safe.

3. **Alternate Nostril Breathing – Finding Emotional Balance**

   - **When to use:** If you feel emotionally exhausted, dissociated, or unable to focus.

   - **Why it works:** This technique balances the left (logical) and right (emotional) sides of the brain, helping you regain clarity and emotional stability.

How to do it:

1. Close your right nostril with your thumb and inhale deeply through the left nostril.

2. Close your left nostril with your ring finger and exhale through the right nostril.

3. Inhale through the right nostril, then switch and exhale through the left nostril.

4. Repeat for 5-10 cycles.

If emotions feel overwhelming, pair this practice with a mantra like "I am safe."

4. Diaphragmatic Breathing – Releasing Emotional Trauma

- ○ **When to use:** When your chest feels tight, your body is tense or you feel trapped in survival mode.
- ○ **Why it works:** This deep breathing technique tells your nervous system that the threat is gone, allowing you to relax.

How to do it:

1. Place one hand on your chest and the other on your belly.
2. Inhale deeply through your nose, making sure your belly (not your chest) rises.
3. Exhale slowly through pursed lips, feeling your belly fall.
4. Repeat for 2-5 minutes.

This is powerful when paired with affirmations like "I am safe now."

5. Humming Bee Breath – Calming Inner Turmoil

- ○ **When to use:** If you feel emotionally overstimulated, restless or disconnected from yourself.
- ○ **Why it works:** The humming sound vibrates through the head and chest, soothing the nervous system and silencing mental noise.

How to do it:

1. Inhale deeply through your nose.
2. As you exhale, make a soft humming "mmmm" sound like a bee.
3. Focus on the vibration in your head and throat.
4. Repeat 5-10 times.

For an even deeper sense of calm, cover your ears while humming to amplify the vibrations.

Breathing is one of the most underrated yet powerful tools for healing. When anxiety strikes or emotions feel uncontrollable, your breath is your anchor— always available, always within reach. Try practicing one or two each day and notice how your body and mind begin to shift.

Key Takeaways

As you finish this book, it's important to revisit the core insights that have been shared. These takeaways can serve as guiding principles in your healing journey and as reminders when navigating relationships moving forward.

1. **Narcissistic Abuse is a Cycle, Not Your Fault:**
   Understanding that narcissistic abuse follows a predictable cycle is crucial. The love-bombing, devaluation and discard phases are not reflections of your worth but tactics designed to control and manipulate you. Their behavior is not your responsibility.

2. **Know Your Worth:**
   Low self-worth often makes individuals more vulnerable to abusive dynamics. Healing begins with acknowledging your inherent value, independent of anyone else's validation or treatment. Learning to prioritize yourself is not selfish- it's survival.

3. **Boundaries are Essential:**
   Setting boundaries is one of the most powerful tools to protect your energy and mental health. Boundaries are not meant to change the narcissist— they are a declaration of what you will and will not accept.

4. **Narcissists Do Not Change:**
   Narcissists lack the self-awareness and accountability required for real change. Therapy often becomes another stage for manipulation, and they are more likely to blame others than to reflect on their own behavior. Acceptance of this reality is liberating.

5. **Emotional Detachment is Key:**
   Whether you're in the process of leaving or have already gone no-contact, emotional detachment is critical. Detachment allows you to protect yourself from their attempts to provoke or guilt you. Remember: their chaos is not your responsibility.

6. **Healing Requires Looking Within:**
   True healing is not about fixing the narcissist but about understanding yourself. Identifying your patterns, addressing past wounds, and building self-worth are the cornerstones of breaking free from toxic cycles.

7. **Trust Your Intuition:**
   Your gut instinct often senses what your mind tries to rationalize away. Trust that inner voice when something feels off. It's your greatest ally in identifying toxic behavior before it can harm you.

8. **Empathy is a Strength, Not a Weakness:**
   Narcissists exploit kindness and empathy, but these traits are not flaws. The key is to balance empathy with discernment, ensuring you don't sacrifice your well-being for someone else's demands.

9. **Growth Through Acceptance and Transformation:**
   Healing is not about "letting go" but about embracing acceptance and surrender. Acceptance means seeing the narcissist and the situation for what they are, without denial or false hope. Surrendering is not about giving up but releasing control over what you cannot change. Transformation happens when you channel your pain into wisdom, strength and a deeper connection with yourself.

10. **Importance of Self-Compassion**
    Self-compassion allows you to embrace your humanity; to recognize that it's okay to feel broken, to make mistakes, and to have moments of weakness. Instead of punishing yourself for what you didn't know or

couldn't do at the time, self compassion reminds you that you did the best you could with the knowledge and resources you had.

11. **Freedom Lies in Self-Rediscovery:**
Freedom doesn't come from external closure or revenge but from rediscovering who you are beneath the trauma. When you reclaim your power, embrace your truth and honor your journey, you become unshakable.

Carry these takeaways with you as you move forward. They are reminders of the power you hold within yourself and the path to a healthier, happier and more fulfilling life.